UCHICAGOCCSR

Foundations for Young Adult Success: A Developmental Framework

⬇ Download the full report at ccsr.uchicago.edu and wallacefoundation.org

This framework synthesizes decades of research evidence, practice wisdom, and theory to capture a holistic view of children's developmental needs from early childhood to young adulthood. Whether at home or school, in an afterschool program, or out in their community, young people are always developing. Broader societal contexts, systems, and institutions shape youth development—often creating big disparities in opportunities and outcomes. Adults also play a pivotal role, and can give young people a better chance at successful lives by understanding and intentionally nurturing their development.

ORGANIZED ACTIVITIES

SCHOOL

SLOW

HOME

Developmental Experiences Can Happen in All Settings

Children are shaped by their interactions with the world, the adults around them, and how they make meaning of their experiences no matter where they are.

Developmental Experiences Require Action and Reflection

Children learn through developmental experiences that combine **Action** *and* **Reflection**, *ideally within the context of trusting relationships with adults.*

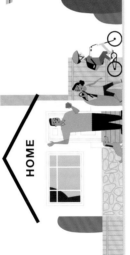

DESCRIBE
EVALUATE
CONNECT
ENVISION
INTEGRATE
ENCOUNTER
TINKER
CHOOSE
PRACTICE
CONTRIBUTE

ACTION
REFLECTION

Developmental Experiences Build Components and Key Factors of Success

Over time, through developmental experiences, children build four foundational components, which underlie three "key factors" to success.

Foundational Components

Self-Regulation includes awareness of oneself and one's surroundings, and managing one's attention, emotions, and behaviors in goal-directed ways.

Knowledge is sets of facts, information, or understanding about self, others, and the world. **Skills** are the learned ability to carry out a task with intended results or goals, and can be either general or domain-specific.

Mindsets are beliefs and attitudes about oneself, the world, and the interaction between the two. They are the lenses we use to process everyday experience.

Values are enduring, often culturally-defined, beliefs about what is good or bad and what is important in life. Values serve as broad guidelines for living and provide an orientation for one's desired future.

Key Factors

Being successful means having the **Agency** to make active choices about one's life path, possessing the **Competencies** to adapt to the demands of different contexts, and incorporating different aspects of oneself into an **Integrated Identity**.

INTEGRATE
VALUES
MINDSETS
REFLECTION
ACTION
SELF-REGULATION
COMPETENCIES
KNOWLEDGE & SKILLS
AGENCY

Funded by The Wallace Foundation

Continued on reverse.

©2015 University of Chicago Consortium on Chicago School Research

MW00386597

UCHICAGO CCSR

Focus of Development Changes as Children Grow Older

Download the full report at ccsr.uchicago.edu and wallacefoundation.org

Providing the right experiences for growth requires knowledge of child and youth development. The development of the four foundational components, along with agency, integrated identity, and competencies, occurs at different stages throughout childhood and adolescence. Development into a successful young adult entails growth of the *self* and one's abilities to interact with *others* and navigate the broader *world*. We define success beyond education and employment to include healthy relationships, a meaningful place within a community, and contributing to a larger good.

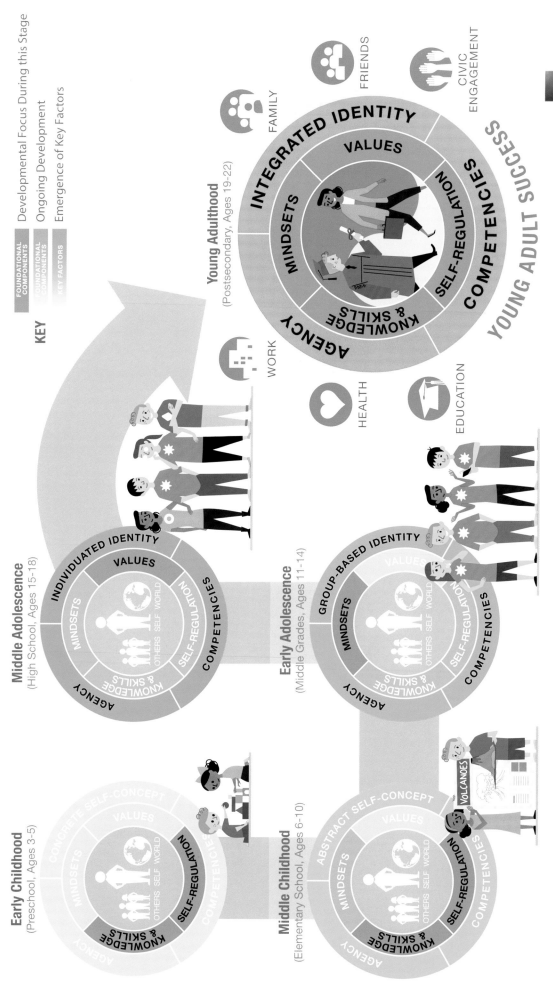

KEY

FOUNDATIONAL COMPONENTS	Developmental Focus During this Stage
FOUNDATIONAL COMPONENTS	Ongoing Development
KEY FACTORS	Emergence of Key Factors

Early Childhood
(Preschool, Ages 3-5)

Middle Childhood
(Elementary School, Ages 6-10)

Early Adolescence
(Middle Grades, Ages 11-14)

Middle Adolescence
(High School, Ages 15-18)

Young Adulthood
(Postsecondary, Ages 19-22)

FAMILY

FRIENDS

CIVIC ENGAGEMENT

WORK

HEALTH

EDUCATION

©2015 University of Chicago Consortium on Chicago School Research

Funded by The Wallace Foundation

Executive Summary

Every society in every age needs to grapple with the question of what outcomes it hopes to produce in raising its young. What exactly do we hope our children will be able to accomplish as adults? What vision guides our work? How do we make that vision a reality for all children? How do we better harness what is known in the research, practice, and policy arenas to ensure that all youth have what they need to successfully meet the complex challenges of young adulthood? Preparing all youth for meaningful, productive futures requires coordinated efforts and intentional practices by adults across all the settings youth inhabit on a daily basis.

To address these questions, this report aims to build a common understanding of young people's developmental needs from early childhood through young adulthood and proposes a developmental framework of the Foundations for Young Adult Success. The framework is the result of synthesizing research, theory, and practice knowledge from a range of disciplines and approaches. This work is influenced by ideas spanning the last century, from Dewey's theory of learning from nearly a century ago to cutting-edge findings in neuroscience on how the brain works. It integrates these perspectives into an accessible framework designed to guide the efforts of all adults who are responsible for raising, educating, or otherwise working with children and youth.

In the past several years, a large number of frameworks and standards have been created to provide guidance on what young people need to learn. The Foundations for Young Adult Success developmental framework describes how to enact these frameworks and standards across the settings in school, out of school, and at home. It characterizes the experiences and relationships youth need to develop into young adults who have agency, an integrated identity, and the requisite competencies to successfully meet the complex challenges of young adulthood and become thriving, contributing members of their communities. The approach described in this report: (1) identifies three key factors of young adult success (agency, an integrated identity, and competencies) and four foundational components (self-regulation, knowledge and skills, mindsets, and values) that underlie them, (2) takes into account what we know about how children develop, (3) considers how the backgrounds of and contexts in which young people live affect their development, and (4) makes the intentional provision of opportunities for young people to experience, interact, and make meaning of their experiences the central vehicle for learning and development.

What Do We Mean by "Success" in Young Adulthood?

Most policy efforts attempt to address socioeconomic gaps in youth outcomes by focusing on educational attainment as the central investment in preparing youth for adulthood. However, while building an educated workforce is one of the core goals of our investments in young people, it is far from the only goal. Success also means that young people can fulfill individual goals and have the agency and competencies to influence the world around them. This broader definition of success is based on the synthesis of literature from various fields, as well as interviews with practice experts and youth service providers (see box entitled *Project Overview and Methodology* p.3), who articulated their larger role as helping young people develop an awareness of themselves and of the wide range of options before them,

1

competencies to pursue those options, and the ability to make good future choices for their lives as engaged citizens in the world. This larger focus is inseparable from goals related to college and career.

Context Plays a Crucial Role in Providing Equal Opportunities to All Youth

The picture of young people as self-actualized masters of destiny is complicated by persuasive research on the role of context in shaping youth outcomes, specifically, structural forces that govern socioeconomic life in the United States (e.g., segregation, discrimination, joblessness).[1] From this perspective, a young person is fundamentally the product of experiences and social interactions, within and across a range of contexts, from the immediate setting to larger institutions to cultural norms, all of which collectively shape the developing individual.[2] Larger contextual factors of society, the economy, and institutions (such as schools) play a central role in the inequitable opportunities afforded to young people, as well as in their ability to see opportunities as viable options and take advantage of them. The obstacles to following a successful path to adulthood and the opportunities available to young adults vary greatly by the contexts they inhabit. Thus, there is a fundamental tension between preparing children to live in the world that is often cast as a tacit acceptance of a profoundly unjust status quo and equipping them to face, navigate, and challenge the inequitable distributions of resources and access that so often limit their opportunities and constrain their potential. It is within these tensions that we explore broad multidisciplinary evidence from research and practice about the underlying constructs that support a successful transition into young adulthood.

Ingredients of "Success" that Comprise the Developmental Framework for Young Adult Success

What are the ingredients necessary for young adults to succeed? Building a common set of objectives and having a clear understanding of how to foster development is a critical step in eliminating the silos that adults working with young people often operate within. To this end, the report provides a framework of foundational components and key factors for success in young adulthood. The report organizes the definition of young adult success around three **key factors**; these are *agency, integrated identity*, and *competencies*. These factors capture how a young adult poised for success interacts with the world (agency), the internal compass that a young adult uses to make decisions consistent with her values, beliefs, and goals (an integrated identity), and how she is able to be effective in different tasks (competencies). The three key factors allow a young adult to manage and adapt to changing demands and successfully navigate various settings with different cultures and expectations. However, a person can have strong agency, identity, and competencies in one setting without being able to automatically transfer those to a new setting; having an *integrated identity* means that a person has consistency and coherence across different roles in different settings.

The Three Key Factors

Agency is the ability to make choices about and take an active role in one's life path, rather than solely being the product of one's circumstances. Agency requires the intentionality and forethought to derive a course of action and adjust course as needed to reflect one's identity, competencies, knowledge and skills, mindsets, and values.

Integrated Identity is a sense of internal consistency of who one is across time and across multiple social identities (e.g., race/ethnicity, profession, culture, gender, religion). An integrated identity serves as an internal framework for making choices and provides a stable base from which one can act in the world.

Competencies are the abilities that enable people to effectively perform roles, complete complex tasks, or achieve specific objectives. Successful young adults have sets of competencies (e.g., critical thinking, responsible decision-making, ability to collaborate) that allow them to be productive and engaged, navigate

---

1   Bowles & Gintis (1976, 2002); Duncan & Murnane (2011); Lewis (2011); Massey & Denton (1993); Putnam (2015); Wilson (1990, 2012).

2   Neal & Neal (2013); Bronfenbrenner (1977, 1979, 1986).

In November 2013, the University of Chicago Consortium on Chicago School Research (UChicago CCSR) was awarded a competitive grant from the Wallace Foundation to build a conceptual framework that articulates what is needed to guide children and youth to become successful young adults. The charge was to analyze and synthesize the best of research evidence, theory, expert opinion, and practice wisdom in the service of identifying the broad range of factors critical for young adult success. We consolidated current understanding of how these factors can be fostered in schools, communities, and homes from early childhood to young adulthood. In addition to a thorough grounding in published research, the project included interviewing and holding convenings and meetings with experts in research, policy, and practice across a range of fields and disciplines. To further ground the synthesis in real-world problems, we also interviewed a diverse selection of nine youth and the adults who work with them in schools, community programs, and agencies in Chicago and developed youth profiles. We sought to find the points of agreement across disparate perspectives, raise the points of contention, and leverage the collective wisdom to best understand the full scope of factors essential to young adult success and how to develop them.

The Three Phases of the Project

To achieve a cohesive and comprehensive framework, the project team undertook three phases of information-gathering. Each successive phase built upon the work of the previous phase, and each phase was defined by a different goal and set of questions:

- **Phase I:** We focused on defining *"success"* and identifying the factors that are critical for success in young adulthood, particularly in college and at the beginning of a career.

- **Phase II:** Building on the critical factors identified in Phase I, we sought to understand how each factor developed over the course of early life, from the preschool years through young adulthood. We focused on the identification of leverage points for best supporting children's holistic development, keeping in mind that child and youth development occurs in multiple settings.

- **Phase III:** We aimed to consolidate current understanding of how critical factors of young adult success can be fostered in a holistic, coordinated way across schools, community organizations, and homes, from early childhood to young adulthood. We focused on a ground-level, practitioner perspective in considering how to best organize adult efforts to promote the development of children and youth.

Each phase of work culminated in internal working documents to help us consolidate our progress and thinking. The white paper that resulted from Phase I, *A Framework for Developing Young Adult Success in the 21st Century: Defining Young Adult Success*, is available at **http://ccsr.uchicago.edu/sites/default/files/publications/Wallace%20Framework%20White%20Paper.pdf**. The current report is a culmination of the three phases of work outlined above, with an emphasis on our learnings from Phases I and II. Findings from Phase III will be explored in future work.

across contexts, perform effectively in different settings, and adapt to different task and setting demands.

The Four Foundational Components

Underlying the capacity for the three key factors are four **foundational components** that span both cognitive and noncognitive factors. These four foundational components are *self-regulation, knowledge and skills, mindsets,* and *values.* The foundational components are developed and expressed in multiple spheres—within the self, in relation to others, and in the broader world(s) one inhabits.[3] The role of each component is threefold. First, when young people have experiences and make meaning of those experiences, each component interacts to promote the development of the other foundational components and the three key factors. Second, they enable healthy and productive functioning at every stage of life. Finally, they directly contribute to young adult

---

3 The notion that positive youth development requires skills in both the interpersonal (or social) and intrapersonal (or self) domains has been put forth by other models and frameworks of skills necessary for success in the 21st century (e.g., Pellegrino & Hilton, 2012; Weissberg & Cascarino, 2013).

success. The foundational components were chosen because they are malleable; that is, they can be changed by experiences and the efforts of and interactions with other people, in both positive and negative ways, and then be internalized. As young people engage in ongoing experiences that help them develop the foundational components, these components can become internalized as automatic responses (or habits) that become a core part of their identity; this automatic behavior allows them to then be transferred across contexts. While all of the foundational components develop throughout every stage of a young person's life, the development of specific components is more salient during some stages than others. Young people develop the foundational components and key factors through experiences and relationships, and these are always embedded within larger societal, economic, and institutional contexts that influence how youth perceive the opportunities and obstacles posed by their environments.

Self-Regulation is the awareness of oneself and one's surroundings, and the ability to manage one's attention, emotions, and behaviors in goal-directed ways. Self-regulation has numerous forms, including cognitive, emotional, behavioral, and attentional regulation. Self-regulation is a key developmental task during early and middle childhood.

Knowledge is the sets of facts, information, or understanding about oneself, others, and the world. Skills are the learned abilities to carry out a task with intended results or goals. Building academic knowledge and skills is a key developmental task during early and middle childhood, although it occurs through all stages of development.

Mindsets are beliefs and attitudes about oneself, the external world, and the interaction between the two. They are the default lenses that individuals use to process everyday experiences. Mindsets reflect a person's unconscious biases, natural tendencies, and past experiences. Though mindsets are malleable, they tend to persist until disrupted and replaced with a different belief or attitude.

Values are enduring, often culturally defined beliefs about what is good or bad, and what is important in life. Values include both the moral code of conduct one uses in daily activities (e.g., being kind, being truthful) and long-term *"outcomes"* of importance (e.g., getting an education, having a family, contributing to the community) that may not necessarily have a right or wrong valence. Values develop through a process of exploration and experimentation, where young people make sense of their experiences and refine what they believe in. Values are a key developmental task during middle adolescence and young adulthood.

Developmental Experiences and Relationships Support Success

Development is a natural, ongoing process that happens as young people observe the world, interact with others, and make meaning of their experiences. Regardless of the degree of adult guidance, children will still *"develop"* in some way, learning how to do things and coming to conclusions about themselves, their prospects, and their paths forward. They will develop some skills and preferences, and they will likely figure out what they need to know to get by. And yet, the developmental benefit of children's experiences can be enhanced and directed by others to help youth best formulate and internalize the developmental *"lessons"* from these experiences.[4] However, the nature and number of children's opportunities for development vary significantly by race and socioeconomic class.

The foundational components and key factors of young adult success are mutually reinforcing, helping young people to both learn from and proactively shape their worlds. The core question for practice is how these foundational components and key factors can be intentionally developed. How do children learn knowledge, skills, values, mindsets, and the complex processes of self-regulation, as well as develop competencies essential to success in the 21st century? The essential social context for this process is what we term **developmental experiences**. Developmental experiences are most supportive of youth's needs when they occur within what the Search Institute calls **developmental**

4

---

4 Vygotsky (1978).

relationships.[5] Development is nurtured in the context of strong, supportive, and sustained developmental relationships with adults and peers. Developmental experiences offer opportunities for young people to engage in various forms of *action* and *reflection*. It is through ongoing cycles of age-appropriate action and reflection experiences that young people build the four foundational components (self-regulation; knowledge and skills; mindsets; and values), and develop agency, an integrated identity, and competencies.

Developmental Experiences

Developmental experiences are opportunities for action and reflection that help young people build self-regulation, knowledge and skills, mindsets, and values, and develop agency, an integrated identity, and competencies. These experiences are *"maximized"* in the context of social interactions with others. Experience must be assigned meaning and be integrated into one's emerging sense of identity if it is to have lasting or transferrable benefit. Mediating young people's thinking about their experience is one important way that adults aid in learning and development.

When young people have the opportunity to make contributions that are valued by others, they gain self-confidence and come to see themselves as capable and able to effect change in their own lives and in the larger world. What matters most for development is not the intentions of adults, but their actual enactment of practices in relation to young people, how young people experience those practices, and the meaning young people make of those experiences. This has training and professional development implications for teachers, parents, childcare providers, and youth workers.

Developmental Relationships

Critical to the process of making meaning out of developmental experiences are strong, supportive, and sustained relationships with caring adults who can encourage young people to reflect on their experiences and help them to interpret those experiences in ways that expand their sense of themselves and their horizons.

The iterative and fundamentally relational processes of experiencing, interacting, and reflecting represent a critical engine for children's development and as such are the core of the conceptual model linking experiences and relationships with outcomes.

Strong, supported, and sustained relationships with caring adults provide an important space for youth to experiment, try out roles and behaviors, and receive feedback that helps to build an integrated identity. However, in order to provide the best experiences for youth, it is imperative to understand where youth are *developmentally* throughout their young lives. This understanding allows for more appropriate interactions between adults and youth. A contextual understanding of children's development offers guidance on how to design direct experiences in ways that provide the right kinds of support and challenges to growth at various stages of early life. Each component develops at different rates over the life course. So when is the most crucial time to be focusing on supporting the maturation of each of our four components? Do they all hold equal weight at different stages of development?

Developmental Progression toward Young Adulthood

Development is multifaceted (social, emotional, attitudinal, behavioral, cognitive, physical) and each aspect of development is inextricably connected to the others. This report takes a developmental perspective because, in order to design and deliver the most effective experiences for youth, it is imperative to understand where youth are developmentally throughout their young lives. This understanding makes it possible for adults to match more appropriate experiences and interactions to the developmental needs of young people.

The practices of adults are more effective when they are intentional, are focused on the foundational components and key factors that support the ability to transition successfully into young adulthood, and are based on an understanding of where youth are developmentally. The development of the key factors of young adult success (competencies, identity, and agency) and

5

---

5   Search Institute (2014).

the four foundational components that underlie them (self-regulation, knowledge and skills, mindsets, and values) occurs at different rates from early childhood through young adulthood. Consistent and supportive interactions with caregivers provide the greatest opportunity for cognitive stimulation, and in ways that can have long-lasting impacts on children's development. Whereas appropriate stimulation supports continuing development, a lack of stimulation can create barriers to later development, potentially requiring more intensive intervention later.

Different factors develop at different rates over the course of life. So when is the most crucial time to be focusing on supporting the maturation of each of the four components or three key factors? Do they all hold equal weight at different stages of development? Below, we highlight the most salient areas of growth during each stage of development, with an eye toward (1) which foundational components or key factors are most influenced by input, experiences, and interactions with others; and (2) which components or key factors need to be developed during the earlier stages to facilitate positive development at later stages. However, it is crucial that adults not exclude other areas of development when engaging with children and youth; nearly every aspect of the foundational components and key factors is forming, or is at least being influenced by the experiences youth encounter, at every stage of life.

In brief, the key developmental tasks during early stages of development are:

- Early childhood (ages 3 to 5): Self-regulation; interpersonal (social-emotional) knowledge and skills

- Middle childhood (ages 6 to 10): Self-regulation (self-awareness and self-control); learning-related skills and knowledge; interpersonal skills

- Early adolescence (ages 11 to 14): Group-based identity; emerging mindsets

- Middle adolescence (ages 15 to 18): Sense of values; individuated identity

- Young adulthood (ages 19 to 22): Integrated identity

What happens as adolescents transition into young adulthood is strongly shaped by the ways in which and degrees to which earlier developmental tasks were met. They draw upon the foundation laid in each preceding stage or the interventions that have successfully compensated for prior developmental lapses. To meet the development tasks as one embarks on young adulthood, a young person should be able to draw upon strong relationships with adults and peers; the foundational components of self-regulation, knowledge and skills, mindsets, and values; and the agency, an integrated identity, and competencies to take an active role in shaping their life course.

Implications for Practice, Policy, and Research

The vision behind the Foundations for Young Adult Success developmental framework is about building a society where all children grow up to reach their full potential, regardless of which side of the economic divide they were born. Currently, opportunities for rich and varied developmental experiences through K-12 schooling and informal education are largely determined by family resources; to address these inequities, it will not be enough to simply expand options by adding more well-run programs, providing a few more resources, or reforming a subset of schools. It will take a transformation of adult beliefs and practices within the existing institutions and structures that shape children's learning and development. It will mean building a collective sense of responsibility for expanding the possibilities for all young people, not just for our own children. It means integrating afterschool providers' lens of youth development with educators' knowledge of learning theory with families' deep understanding of the unique needs and circumstances of their children. By drawing from the knowledge, approaches, and experience of many different adults from many different settings, we can give the next generation of young people the opportunities they need to meet their full potential.

The Foundations for Young Adult Success developmental framework has clear implications for schools, youth organizations, and families; but without larger transformations in the policy landscape and larger societal and economic context, there are limits to what can be achieved. Many questions remain about how to more effectively support the development of young people and what policies and structural changes are needed; these form the basis for the research agenda needed to guide these transformations. Along with parents and families, the world we envision for the next generation of young people will require the joint efforts of educators and youth practitioners, policymakers, and researchers. Below we provide implications for teachers, youth practitioners, parents and families, policymakers, and researchers.

Implications for Educators, Youth Practitioners, and Parents and Families

1. A narrow focus on content knowledge in isolation from the other foundational components undermines learning and development. Learning and development are holistic processes dependent on interactions among all of the foundational components (self-regulation, knowledge and skills, mindsets, and values). There may be conceptual reasons for distinguishing between *"cognitive"* and *"noncognitive"* factors, but this distinction has no functional meaning. Cognition, emotion, affect, and behavior are reflexive, mutually reinforcing, and inextricably associated with one another as a part of development and learning. Adults will make little headway if they target only one particular component or subcomponent in isolation.

2. Taking a developmental lens is essential to ensuring that structures and practices meet the developmental needs of the young people being served. Although a lot is known about development, too often, there is a mismatch between the structures or practices in a youth setting and the developmental needs of the young people being served. Schools, youth programs, and even families are too often oriented to adult needs and goals (e.g., maintaining classroom discipline) instead of taking a youth-centered approach.

3. Ensuring all young people have access to a multitude of rich developmental experiences is imperative to their success. Growing up in marginalized communities adds to the complexity of developing into a young adult who is poised for success. While having agency equips young people to make choices and take action, their ability to successfully pursue a desired path also depends on social relationships, financial resources, and countless other external factors that are inequitably distributed. Further, the task of *"integrating"* one's identity is vastly more complicated for low-income youth and youth of color than it is for children who grow up within the social and behavioral norms of the dominant white, middle-class culture.[6] Responding to this reality requires a careful balance of pragmatism and aspiration. The Foundations for Young Adult Success developmental framework is designed to strike a balance between helping youth thrive in the world as it is, and develop the skills and dispositions they need to challenge a profoundly unjust status quo.[7]

Implications for Education and Youth Policy

1. The current policy emphasis on content knowledge and test-based accountability undermines practitioners' ability to provide developmental experiences. Content knowledge is an essential part of what young people need to learn for the future, whether in school, at home, or in afterschool programs, but it is far from the only thing that matters. Policies that put too great an emphasis on content knowledge and standardized tests create incentives for practitioners to see the teaching of content knowledge as the sole outcome of interest. As this report has shown, the other foundational components not only facilitate engagement and learning of content knowledge, but they also are important developmental outcomes in and of themselves. Policies that promote these other foundational components would help to create conditions that foster both the learning of academic content and the development of young people more holistically.

---

6 Deutsch (2008); Fedelina Chávez & Guido-DiBrito (1999); Phinney (1989); Phinney & Rosenthal (1992).

7 This report does not directly address how development of the key factors and foundational components may play out differently for different groups (e.g., by gender, sexual orientation, immigrant status, involvement in the juvenile justice system) and what specific barriers, assets, and needs each subgroup may have. This is a critical area of investigation that should be pursued.

2. Proceed carefully with incorporating *"noncognitive"* measures into accountability systems. The policy window for a more holistic approach to the development and learning of young people is opening; there is growing discontent over standardized testing. Recently, a movement to integrate alternative measures of student success into school accountability systems has gained some momentum, exemplified by the California *"CORE"* districts that have received No Child Left Behind waivers allowing them to include social-emotional factors and school climate measures in place of test scores as accountability metrics. This holistic approach to evaluating students is in alignment with the Foundations for Young Adult Success developmental framework; however, some caution is necessary when using these new measures for accountability purposes. Many important questions remain about measuring noncognitive or social-emotional factors and about their suitability for an accountability system that was developed around standardized tests.[8]

3. Policy needs to provide the *"safe space"* for schools and out-of-school programs to become learning organizations. The ambitious vision given in the Foundations for Young Adult Success developmental framework does not provide a clear roadmap of specific practices, strategies, or programs to implement. Moving from the current approach to schooling to a more holistic and developmentally aligned approach will require trial and error. Just as young people need opportunities to tinker and practice in order to learn, practitioners also need opportunities for tinkering and practicing, as well as making mistakes, as they learn new ways of teaching and working with young people. In an age when accountability is a dominant way of managing schools, and increasingly out-of-school programs as well, the space to make mistakes is very small. For real shifts to happen in practice, schools and out-of-school programs need to become learning organizations that provide opportunities for adults to learn, and policy needs to provide the *"safe space"* to do so.

Gaps in the Research

1. What practices and strategies promote the development of identity and agency? While researchers have learned a tremendous amount about development in the last several decades, many questions remain unanswered. In this report, we provided a developmental trajectory for the key factors for young adult success—agency, an integrated identity, and competencies. However, this relied on piecing together a number of existing theories; rarely if ever has the development of agency, for example, been studied longitudinally from early childhood through young adulthood. Theory has provided guidance on how an early sense of *"self"* underlies later identity formation, but this area is understudied in empirical research. While there is converging evidence that supports each of the developmental experiences we identify in this report, as well as the importance of developmental relationships, we do not know which specific combination of experiences would best promote the formation of an integrated identity and agency. We also still lack a strong understanding of how all of the foundational components outlined here link directly to the development of agency, an integrated identity, and competencies.

2. What can be done to intervene with young people after developmental windows close? The Foundations for Young Adult Success developmental framework includes four foundational components— self-regulation, knowledge and skills, mindsets, and values—which are all crucial factors in a person's development toward optimal capacity. What happens if youth do not grow each of these foundational components in the developmental period during which they are most malleable? What types of interventions should we invest in—and for whom and at what period in their lives—if children seem to be falling behind? And for the youngest children, how can we even be sure that a child is falling outside of *"normative"* development, given how very wide the range of development is during the early years?

---

8 See Duckworth & Yeager (2015) for a discussion of the uses and limitations of existing measures.

3. **What is the interaction of experiences in different settings?** This report also raises a number of questions about the experiences youth encounter in the various settings they inhabit on a daily basis. We know quite well that what youth experience in school often varies from their experiences with friends, at home, or even in other educational settings. What we do not know is the extent to which those experiences need to be coordinated and supportive of each other, even if they are not teaching the same skills. How much do practices at home support or inhibit what teachers, youth workers, and others aim to do with youth? How aligned do those practices need to be? And can effective practices in one setting ameliorate negative experiences in another setting?

4. **How can the key factors and foundational components best be measured for different purposes?** Measurement is a core part of evaluating needs and gauging progress in any field. With the growing interest in factors other than academic content knowledge and skills, the number of assessments created to measure these factors has also grown. As discussed in the policy implications section, a number of questions about these factors and the assessments complicate their immediate implementation into practice. Some key questions include: Is this factor best conceived as an individual characteristic that can be cultivated over time or as a situational response to particular settings, opportunities, or expectations? How can we disentangle young people's prior capacities from changes induced by setting factors such as adult practice, opportunities for developmental relationships and developmental experiences, or the culture and climate of the place? What is the developmental trajectory on these measures and what are thresholds for what young people need?

In short, the demand for measures of noncognitive or social-emotional factors has far outpaced the state of the field of measurement for these same constructs. In a case such as this, there is great potential for measurement instruments to be misused, to produce faulty data, to conflate statistical significance with meaningfulness, or to otherwise lead practitioners down a fruitless path. We strongly urge caution in the use of measurement tools until the science of measuring these important constructs catches up with the interest in and demand for them.

Conclusion

The Foundations for Young Adult Success developmental framework is a first step in guiding practitioners, policymakers, parents, and researchers in working together around a vision of building a society where all children grow up to reach their full potential regardless of differences in their backgrounds. Ensuring that young people grow into successful young adults requires investments in their learning and development from birth to young adulthood so that all of them have ongoing opportunities to truly reach their potential.

Making this vision a reality will require a collective responsibility for all young people. It means asking practitioners to question their own beliefs about what is possible and rethink how they work with young people on a day-to-day basis. It means asking policymakers to focus on a bigger picture and broader set of outcomes and to consider policies that would support the efforts of practitioners in developing young people. It means asking researchers to provide accessible, meaningful, and actionable answers to core questions of policy and practice. It means asking families to understand the needs of their children and work with the institutions they cross everyday so that these needs are met. It means asking for change within existing institutions and structures while also asking what new institutions and structures might better serve our vision. Addressing the inequities of opportunities facing young adults will require more than equipping young people with the capacity to navigate the world as it exists now, it will mean that they are also able to envision and create a better world for future generations.

9

INTRODUCTION

Defining Success in Young Adulthood

Every society in every age needs to grapple with the question of what outcomes it hopes to produce in raising its young. This seems particularly critical for adults who devote their lives to improving children's education and development. What exactly do we hope our children will be able to accomplish as adults? What vision guides our work? How do we make that vision a reality for all children?

As a nation we make enormous investments in our youth. But for many young people, inequities in the distribution of resources and social and economic barriers mean that they will not reach their full potential. How do we better harness what is known in the research, practice, and policy arenas to ensure that all youth have what they need to successfully meet the complex challenges of young adulthood and become thriving, contributing members of their communities?

To address these questions, this report aims to build a common understanding of young people's developmental needs from early childhood through young adulthood. Preparing *all* youth for meaningful, productive futures requires coordinated efforts and intentional practices by adults across the many settings youth inhabit on a daily basis—whether in school, at home, or in organized community programs.[9] Building off of previous frameworks and literature reviews,[10] this report provides a new synthesis of knowledge gathered through a review of the literature and interviews of experts from youth development, psychology, sociology, pediatrics, economics, education, and the cognitive sciences to generate the Foundations for Young Adult

Success developmental framework (**see Figure 1**), which depicts what youth need to be prepared for adulthood. It utilizes ideas from well-established theorists such as John Dewey and Erik Erikson to cutting-edge findings from neuroscience about how people learn. This report incorporates a wide array of evidence to highlight the types of experiences adults should provide for youth to help them in developing to their full potential.

In this report we focus on the key role that developmental experiences and developmental relationships play in supporting a child's long-term success, while keeping in mind variations in children's individual development over time. Young people's needs and capabilities change as they grow up, and attending to their ongoing development is an essential part of supporting youth. In bringing all of these pieces together, this report recognizes that young people inhabit a multitude of settings on a daily basis where they develop, grow, and learn, and that broader societal contexts, systems, and institutions also shape youth development—often creating big disparities in opportunities and outcomes. Our focus here is on the experience of children growing up in the United States in the early 21st century.[11] We

---

9 Hill, Campbell, & Harvey (2000); Irby, Pittman, & Tolman (2003).

10 For example, Farrington et al. (2012); National Research Council and Institute of Medicine (2002); Pellegrino & Hinton (2012).

11 While some aspects of child and adolescent development may be common across different countries, cultures, or time periods, we are not making claims that the findings or framework apply outside of the experience of young people in the United States in the early 21st century.

FIGURE 1

UChicago CCSR Framework for What Youth Need to Make a Successful Transition to Adulthood

Developmental Experiences Can Happen in All Settings

HOME   SCHOOL   ORGANIZED ACTIVITIES

Over time, through developmental experiences, children build four foundational components, which underlie three "key factors" to success.

Developmental Experiences Require Action and Reflection

CONTRIBUTE   DESCRIBE
PRACTICE   EVALUATE
ACTION
CHOOSE   CONNECT
REFLECTION
TINKER   ENVISION
ENCOUNTER   INTEGRATE

Foundational Components

Self-Regulation includes awareness of oneself and one's surroundings, and managing one's attention, emotions, and behaviors in goal-directed ways.

Knowledge is sets of facts, information, or understanding about self, others, and the world. **Skills** are the learned ability to carry out a task with intended results or goals, and can be either general or domain-specific.

Mindsets are beliefs and attitudes about oneself, the world, and the interaction between the two. They are the lenses we use to process everyday experience.

Values are enduring, often culturally-defined, beliefs about what is good or bad and what one thinks is important in life. Values serve as broad guidelines for living and provide an orientation for one's desired future.

Key Factors

Being successful means having the **Agency** to make active choices about one's life path, possessing the **Competencies** to adapt to the demands of different contexts, and incorporating different aspects of oneself into an **Integrated Identity**.

---

hope that a common understanding of the needs and strengths of young people will encourage coordinated efforts and intentional practices by adults across settings, enabling a more cohesive system of supports for healthy development, better preparing young people from all walks of life for productive futures.

Defining "Success" in Young Adulthood

With rising income inequality, the gap in the investments that families of differing income levels are able to make in their children has widened.[12] As a result, the experiences and opportunities young people have to grow and develop vary greatly by the circumstances they are born into. Most policy efforts attempt to address socioeconomic gaps in outcomes by focusing on educational attainment as the central investment in preparing youth for adulthood. This approach has yielded some gains; national high school completion rates have risen to 80 percent, but there continue to be gaps by race/ethnicity and income. Eighty-six percent of white students complete high school compared to

73 percent and 69 percent, for Latinos and African Americans, respectively, and 72 percent for economically disadvantaged students.[13] Furthermore, having a high school diploma does not ensure employment, and the economic prospects are dim for those without a post-secondary degree or training. Disparities in higher education, combined with the effects of economic inequality, disadvantaged neighborhoods, unstable labor markets, and troubled K-12 schools, mean that a large percentage of youth—particularly those in low-income and racial/ethnic minority communities—face a future with starkly diminished economic opportunities.[14]

Given the harsh economic prospects facing youth with limited education, school reformers and policymakers have argued that it is not enough for American students to earn a high school diploma; they must be prepared to continue their education to and through college.[15] College completion has become the marker not just for individual success, but for the country as a whole. In the context of waning American advantage in a competitive global marketplace, the education policy narrative is

---

12 Chetty et al. (2014a), Chetty et al. (2014b); Reardon (2011).
13 Stetser & Stillwell (2014).
14 Bureau of Labor Statistics (2013); Duncan & Murnane (2011).
15 Achieve, Inc. (2012); Education Trust (2012).

12

often framed in terms of developing workers for 21st century jobs. In President Obama's words, *"America cannot lead in the 21st century unless we have the best educated, most competitive workforce in the world."*[16]

Building an educated workforce is one of the core goals of our investments in young people, but it is far from the only goal. Our investments shape the contributions future adults can make to their families and communities, their ability to engage in civic life, and how they view their role in society. Particularly when we move from the perspective of the policymaker to that of a parent, we would define success for our children beyond just college and career. We want our children to be happy, healthy, and confident in themselves, and to have whatever preparation they need to become caring adults with meaningful work, family and friends who love them, and a strong connection to the community. This broader developmental perspective is often shared by teachers, counselors, afterschool providers, coaches, ministers, scout leaders, arts educators, and other youth workers. We interviewed many of these practice experts as part of this report (**see box entitled** *Project Overview and Methodology* **on p.17**), and found that people in these professions generally value the unique gifts that youth bring to the world and want to help children and teenagers realize their own potential across multiple spheres. This belief was articulated by many of the experts we talked with as we began this project:

> Our ultimate goal for the students we serve is simple. By age 25, we expect [them] to be capable of making real choices to pursue the life and career they want to lead. In other words, the end goal is agency. It's what I— as a parent—want for my daughter. We want the same exact thing for the students we work with today. We don't care if our alumni choose to be doctors, or teachers, or politicians, but we do intend to ensure they have the capacity to do what they independently want to do. —Jeff Nelson, CEO, OneGoal[17]

Educators and youth service providers recognize that getting an education and a job are critically important outcomes; however, they generally have a much broader conception of the goals of their work—and what the measures of success ought to be. Regardless of the specific mission of the organization in which they work, these adults often articulated their larger role as helping young people develop an awareness of themselves and of the wide range of options before them, competencies to pursue those options, and the ability to make good future choices for their lives as engaged citizens in the world. This larger focus is inseparable from goals related to college and career. Thus, young adult success potentially encompasses different meanings for different people and background, culture, values, and geography shape an individual's definition of a successful life.

Going to college or other post-secondary training, particularly for students with no other access to well-paying work, has a core role in young adult success for many people, but self-advancement is only part of the story of young adult success. *"Success"* goes beyond fulfilling individual goals and extends to having the agency and competencies to influence the world. We need to develop facile thinkers, inventors, and problem-solvers with not only deep content knowledge, but also the creativity and flexibility to apply their knowledge to novel situations.[18] We need to prepare young people to address global challenges and alleviate human suffering.[19] So too do we want to develop thoughtful and informed citizens who can continue to pursue the ideals of democracy that have led our country for almost 250 years. From this perspective, preparing adolescents for adulthood means cultivating young people's critical thinking skills, building their knowledge of democratic institutions and processes, and nurturing in them a sense of service to their communities and engagement in the political process.[20] The conception of success we use in this report thus has both an individual and a societal element. It is not simply about meeting one's own goals; success is also about contributing to a larger good, having a meaningful place within a community, and working toward a positive change in the world.

13

---

16 The U.S. White House, Remarks on Higher Education, April 24, 2009.

17 UChicago CCSR interview with Jeff Nelson, CEO, OneGoal, January 14, 2014.

18 Pellegrino & Hilton (2012).

19 Wagner & Compton (2012).

20 Gould (2011); U.S. Department of Education (2012).

What Leads to Adult Success?

To fulfill this broader definition of success, the question is not only what courses students should take in school, what test scores they need, or what facts or formulas they ought to know, but also what kinds of experiences young people need to prepare them to meet both inward-looking goals for creating a meaningful life and more outward-facing goals such as getting a good job or contributing to their communities.

In this report, we define a person who is ready to make a successful transition into young adulthood as having three key factors: the **agency** to take an active role in shaping one's path, the ability to incorporate different aspects of oneself into an **integrated identity**, and the **competencies** needed to effectively navigate a range of social contexts. Having agency means having the ability to make choices and take an active role in managing one's life path, rather than being solely the product of one's circumstances. This definition of agency acknowledges that external factors form very real constraints, and also that people have the will and the power to influence external factors and can make choices about how to respond to constraints. Having an integrated identity means having a core sense of who one is, including a sense of continuity with one's past and future possibilities. Competencies are the abilities that enable people to effectively perform roles, complete complex tasks, or achieve specific objectives to achieve success. Young adults require competencies in order to adapt to the demands of different settings and be productive and effective within them.

Developing the three key factors of agency, an integrated identity, and competencies in multiple contexts is likely to be a lifelong endeavor, but their foundations lie in childhood and adolescence. Adolescence is the last stage of major developmental growth and is often the time of the last interaction with the education system; as young people enter young adulthood they begin to navigate the larger world and meet milestones such as

entering the workforce, getting married, having children, or moving to a new community. Thus the development of these three key factors is the central task of raising and educating young people to prepare them for the life changes that can begin in young adulthood.

What are the components that underlie the development of agency, integrated identity, and competencies? Through a review of the literature and interviews with experts, we have identified four foundational components that are precursors to the key factors of young adult success. We have included both cognitive and noncognitive factors in the foundational components. James Heckman's initial conceptualization of the role of noncognitive factors in adult outcomes greatly furthered our understanding of what contributes to young adult success.[21] However, emphasizing a separation between cognitive and noncognitive factors does little to illuminate *how* to effectively prepare young people for future success; cognitive and noncognitive factors interact with each other to contribute to learning and growth.

Many frameworks of competencies and cognitive and noncognitive factors have been put forth in recent years. The foundational components presented here provide broad categories that organize and underlie the elements of these existing frameworks. Thus, the Foundations for Young Adult Success developmental framework is designed to help translate these different elements into an action plan for development, rather than to supplant other frameworks.

The four foundational components are: **self-regulation, knowledge and skills, mindsets, and values**. Self-regulation includes awareness of oneself and one's surroundings, and the management of one's attention, emotions, and behaviors in goal-directed ways. Knowledge comprises sets of facts, information, or understandings about the self, others, and the world. Skills are the learned ability to carry out a task with intended results or goals, and can be either general or domain-specific. Mindsets are beliefs and attitudes about oneself and the external world; they are the default lenses we use to process everyday experience. Values are lasting

14

---

21 Heckman & Rubinstein (2001).

ideas or principles, often culturally defined, about what is good or bad and what one considers important in life. Values serve as broad guidelines for living and provide an orientation for one's desired future.

Each of the foundational components plays an important role in the development and enactment of an integrated identity, agency, and competencies.

Context Plays a Crucial Role in Providing Equal Opportunities to All Youth

The inspiring picture of young people as self-actualized masters of destiny is complicated by persuasive research on the role of context in shaping youth outcomes, specifically, structural forces that govern socioeconomic life in the United States (e.g., segregation, discrimination, joblessness).[22] From this perspective, a young person is fundamentally the product of his experiences and social interactions; he is subject to cultural norms, within and across a range of contexts, from the immediate setting to larger institutions, all of which collectively shape the developing individual and the options before him.[23] These larger contextual factors of society, the economy, and institutions (such as schools) play a central role in the inequitable opportunities afforded to young people, as well as in their ability to see opportunities as viable options and to take advantage of them. While having agency equips young adults to make choices and take action, the ability to pursue a desired path also depends on social relationships, financial resources, and countless other external factors that are inequitably distributed. Thus, youth growing up in marginalized communities have grossly different opportunities to build skills and competence, and their options for the future may be severely constrained. Further, the task of *"integrating"* one's identity is vastly more complicated for low-income youth and youth of color as they interact with the cultural and behavioral norms of a dominant white, middle-class culture than it is for children who grow up within that culture.[24] The obstacles to following a successful path to adulthood and the opportunities available to young adults vary greatly by the contexts they inhabit; these limitations are a critical part of the story of education and development.

Thus, there is a fundamental tension between preparing children to live in the world that is—which is often cast as a tacit acceptance of a profoundly unjust status quo—and equipping them to face, navigate, and challenge the inequitable distributions of resources and access that so often limit their opportunities and constrain their potential. While adults need to be pragmatic in their work with kids and acknowledge the inequities in opportunities afforded youth, they should also be aspirational. How can we design and enact practices with schools, youth organizations, families, and communities that not only prepare young people for the *"real world,"* but that also inspire and equip them to create a better world? How can we ensure that *all* youth develop a repertoire of competencies that would enable them to confront injustice and work toward a more inclusive society? At the heart of this project has been the vision of young adults with an integrated identity, with the agency to actively shape their life path, and the competencies that allow them to pursue both individual and larger social goals, and who have developed deep relationships with friends, family, and the community. While teachers, parents, and other youth workers must recognize and prepare young people for the real constraints they will face in society, we should not be content to merely prepare youth to fill a slot in the world that is.

It is within these tensions that we explore a rich theoretical tradition and broad multidisciplinary evidence from research and practice about the underlying constructs that support a successful transition into young adulthood. We approach this by considering how well the key factors for young adult success would equip young people from under-resourced communities to navigate complex institutional environments and confront structural inequalities.

To that end, Chapter 1 provides an extensive overview of the key factors for young adult success and the foundational components underlying them. The

15

22 Bowles & Gintis (1976, 2002); Duncan & Murnane (2011); Lewis (2011); Massey & Denton (1993); Putnam (2015); Wilson (1990, 2012).

23 Neal & Neal (2013); Bronfenbrenner (1977, 1979, 1986).

24 Deutsch (2008); Fedelina Chávez & Guido-DiBrito (1999); Phinney (1989); Phinney & Rosenthal (1992).

chapter starts with an in-depth discussion of *agency, integrated identity,* and *competencies,* and addresses *why* these factors are crucial to creating and maintaining a productive and satisfying adult life; these three factors serve as our *"north star"* throughout the report. We then describe and review each of foundational component that underlies these key factors, making a case for why each component is considered foundational in the development of agency and integrated identity as well as in supporting competency development. In Chapter 2, we focus on *how* these foundational components can be nurtured in childhood and adolescence, with an emphasis on *developmental experiences* set within the context of *developmental relationships.* Chapter 3 addresses the question of *when* the foundational components and key factors develop, as we look at key developmental tasks from early childhood to young adulthood (ages 3 to 22). In the final chapter, we summarize the implications of this framework for practice, policy, and research. Throughout the remainder of this report, we open each chapter with the key points of the chapter.

16

In November 2013, the University of Chicago Consortium on Chicago School Research (UChicago CCSR) was awarded a competitive grant from the Wallace Foundation to build a conceptual framework that articulates what is needed to guide children and youth to become successful young adults. The charge was to analyze and synthesize the best of research evidence, theory, expert opinion, and practice wisdom in the service of identifying the broad range of factors critical for young adult success. We were to consolidate current understanding of how these factors can be fostered in schools, communities, and homes from early childhood to young adulthood. In addition to a thorough grounding in published research, our work involved talking to experts in research and practice across a range of fields and disciplines. We sought to find the points of agreement across disparate perspectives, raise the points of contention, and leverage the collective wisdom of diverse lines of research, practice, and theory to best understand the full scope of factors essential to young adult success.

The Three Phases of the Project

To achieve a cohesive and comprehensive framework, the project team undertook three phases of information-gathering, with each successive phase built upon the work of the previous one. Each phase was defined by a different goal and set of questions:

- **Phase I:** We focused on defining "success" and identifying the factors that are critical for success in young adulthood, particularly in college and at the beginning of a career. Questions included:

  1. What does a successful young adult look like?

  2. What characteristics, attitudes, skills, and behaviors help people succeed in typical young adult settings?

  3. What institutional, societal, and economic forces should we consider as we develop a framework for the critical factors needed to promote young adult success?

- **Phase II:** Building on the critical factors identified in Phase I, we sought to understand how each factor developed over the course of early life, from the preschool years through young adulthood. We focused on the identification of leverage points for best supporting children's holistic development, keeping in mind that child and youth development occurs in multiple settings. Questions included:

1. How do the critical factors identified in Phase I develop from early childhood through young adulthood?

2. What are the most salient areas of development during each stage of early life based on research and practice knowledge of *"normative"* development?

3. What do we know about the roles that youth's environments and important others (including caregivers and other adults) play in supporting successful development during each stage of development?

- **Phase III:** We aimed to consolidate current understanding of how critical factors of young adult success can be fostered in a holistic, coordinated way across schools, community organizations, and homes, from early childhood to young adulthood. We focused on a ground-level, practitioner perspective in considering how to best organize adult efforts to promote the development of children and youth. Our work during this phase focused on the following key questions:

1. What are the key setting components and experiences youth need to support the development of each factor in each stage of life?

2. What should adults consider as they are designing effective practice with developing youth?

3. How do intentional practices interact with youth experiences to lead to positive development and learning?

Methods

During each phase, the team used several modes of information-gathering. First, we analyzed and synthesized the best theory and empirical evidence, focusing on highly-cited research and recommended publications. As part of this work, we reviewed over 20 existing models and frameworks that focus on *"noncognitive"* factors, inter- and intra-personal competencies, and social-emotional skills in adolescence and young adulthood. Second, we interviewed and held meetings with research and practice experts with specific knowledge in areas related to each phase of our work (**see Appendix** for a list of names). These experts included researchers from different fields and disciplines (e.g., psychology, business, education, sociology, economics) as well as policymakers and practitioners from a range of organizations (e.g.,

17

programs and providers focusing on college access and support, workforce development, K-12 education, after-school and extended learning time, community connections with schools, early childhood, and family support services). These experts were identified through our literature review, as well as through our professional networks in academia and the practice realm. We also interviewed experts who were recommended to us by our original interviewees. Third, we continuously synthesized research and interview data in weekly group meetings to determine the points of agreement and points of contention across disparate perspectives. Fourth, we held a number of meetings throughout the project, including two larger convenings of research and practice experts to evaluate and offer feedback to advance our work. We incorporated this feedback to improve the framework and our synthesis. Fifth, we interviewed nine diverse youth and the adults who work with them in schools, community programs, and agencies in Chicago. We used these interviews to highlight developmental experiences and surface real-life challenges young people are facing as they navigate across contexts. We also wrote biographical profiles from these interviews to illustrate how youth create narratives about their experiences. The youth profiles further informed our model.

Each phase of work culminated in internal working documents to help us consolidate our progress and thinking. The white paper that resulted from Phase I, *A Framework for Developing Young Adult Success in the 21st Century: Defining Young Adult Success*, is available at **http://ccsr.uchicago.edu/sites/default/files/publications/Wallace%20Framework%20White%20Paper.pdf**

The current report is a culmination of the three phases of work outlined above, with an emphasis on our learnings from Phases I and II. Findings from Phase III will be more fully explored in future work. We present here our conceptualization of *"success"* in young adulthood, our resultant conceptual framework of foundational components and key factors for success in young adulthood, implications for practice in a range of settings in which children and youth spend their time, gaps in the existing knowledge and literature, and future directions for research. We designed this final report as an actionable document that can organize and guide the strategic direction and inform the daily work of practitioners and policymakers.

18

What are the Ingredients of "Success"?

Key Points

- Success in young adulthood depends on more than *"college and career"* success; a definition of success should include the multi-faceted ways individuals may seek meaning in life and contribute to the world.

- We organize the definition of young adult success around three **key factors**; these are *agency, integrated identity,* and *competencies*—and four **foundational components** that underlie them: *self-regulation, knowledge and skills, mindsets,* and *values.*

- The role of the foundational components is threefold: when young people have experiences and make meaning of those experiences, each component interacts to promote the development of the other foundational components and the three key factors; they enable healthy and productive functioning at every stage of life; and they directly contribute to young adult success.

- The four foundational components and three key factors are closely interrelated in supporting how young people act in the world and make meaning of an experience. Understanding this interrelationship can help adults provide integrative opportunities for youth to act and reflect in ways that make the most of developmental experiences, rather than targeting only one particular component or factor in isolation.

- Noncognitive and cognitive factors should not be considered independently; they interact with each other to promote and mutually reinforce development and learning. Both are a core part of how students learn.

- The experiences that youth encounter are always embedded within larger societal, economic, and institutional contexts that influence how youth perceive the opportunities and obstacles posed by their environments.

What are the ingredients necessary for young adults to succeed? Building a common set of objectives and having a clear understanding of how to foster development is a critical step in eliminating the silos that adults working with young people often operate within. This project proposes a framework of foundational components and key factors for success in young adulthood. Drawing from a review of the literature, both empirical and theoretical, and the knowledge of a wide range of expert contributors, this report organizes the definition of young adult success around three **key factors**; these are *agency, integrated identity,* and *competencies.* These factors capture how a young adult poised for success interacts with the world (agency), the internal compass that a young adult uses to make decisions consistent with her values, beliefs, and goals (integrated identity), and how she is able to be effective in differ-

ent tasks (competencies). The three key factors allow a young adult to manage and adapt to changing demands and successfully navigate various settings with different cultures and expectations. While recognizing the economic imperative of going to college, particularly for youth with no other access to well-paying work, we define success in young adulthood beyond the more narrow notion of *"college and career"* success to acknowledge and embrace the multi-faceted ways individuals may seek meaning in life and contribute to the world. Adolescent psychiatrists Hazen, Schlozman, and Beresin have described the successful culmination of adolescence as resulting in *"a biologically mature individual equipped with a sense of an independent self, the capacity to form close peer and group relationships, and the cognitive and psychological resources to face the challenges of adult life."* [25]

---

25 Hazen, Scholzman, & Beresin (2008, p. 167).

At the core of this project is a vision of young adults who, regardless of where they grow up, meet the challenges and joys of life with agency, possess an integrated identity that gives them a core sense of who they are, and have the competencies that allow them to pursue both individual and larger social goals. These three key factors allow a young adult to accomplish a wide range of goals, including achieving success in school or work, maintaining a physically and psychologically healthy lifestyle, and having deep relationships with friends, family, and other community members. In this chapter, we focus on the transition from adolescence into young adulthood. We explore both these key factors of young adult success and the foundational components that underlie them, which are the outcomes of interest in our Foundations for Young Adult Success developmental framework (**see Figure 2**).

As this chapter will articulate, a successful transition into young adulthood will be supported by the three key factors outlined above. We want to clarify, however, that a person can have agency, integrated identity, and competencies in one setting without being able to automatically transfer those to a new setting. A young woman might enter young adulthood with a strong identity and a set of competencies that allow her to act with agency in one role or setting (for example, as a songwriter who performs at regular open-mics), but lack the identity and competencies to act with agency in another role or setting (for example, as a college student). High school students might likewise exhibit persistence and strong academic performance in a high school setting and then essentially fall apart when they go off to college. Indeed, educators in successful urban high schools have often expressed frustration at the difficulty of getting students' confidence and good habits developed in high school to transfer to post-secondary settings. Ultimately, then, the task at hand for adults who work with youth is to help young people not only build their agency, identity, and competencies in specific domains, but also help them to leverage these strengths from one arena and transfer them to tackle challenges in new contexts.

Underlying the capacity for the three key factors are four **foundational components**—a set of both cognitive and noncognitive factors. The four foundational components are *self-regulation, knowledge and skills,*

mindsets, and *values.* The role of each of these foundational components is threefold. First, when young people have experiences and make meaning of those experiences, each component interacts to promote the development of the other foundational components and the three key factors. Second, they enable healthy and productive functioning at every stage of life. Finally, they directly contribute to young adult success. The foundational components develop as they are used. Over time, self-regulation, knowledge and skills, mindsets, and values can become internalized as lenses for seeing the world or as automatic responses (or habits) that become a core part of one's identity; this automatic behavior supports the transfer of these foundational components across contexts. We elaborate on the four foundational components later in this chapter.

20

FIGURE 2

Key Factors and Foundational Components for Young Adult Success

Key Factors

Agency

At the heart of successful young adulthood is the concept of agency. **Agency** means taking an active and intentional role in making choices and shaping and managing the course of one's life rather than being at the mercy of external forces. Agency is reliant on having an internal locus of control—the belief that you have control over what happens to you in life.[26] Having agency also requires having the competencies to be able to manage one's environment, a sense of what one values, the ability to manage one's emotions and behavior, as well as a belief that conscious self-directed action is possible. Philosopher Isaiah Berlin further elucidated this concept:

> [To be a rational agent is] to be a subject, not an object; to be moved by reasons, by conscious purposes, which are my own, not by causes which affect me, as it were, from outside. I wish to be somebody, not nobody; a doer—deciding, not being decided for, self-directed and not acted upon by external nature or by other men as if I were a thing, or an animal, or a slave incapable of playing a human role, that is, of conceiving goals and policies of my own and realizing them.... I wish, above all, to be conscious of myself as a thinking, willing, active being, bearing responsibility for my choices and able to explain them by reference to my own ideas and purposes.[27]

When young people, particularly those from marginalized communities, engage with the world, their capacity to act with agency is constrained and shaped by a number of factors, from the opportunities that are presented to them, to how others react to them, to their own competencies. Agency allows one to confront the challenges and barriers that are encountered in life, not as fixed limits to what is possible, but as obstacles that can be overcome.

The individual expression of agency is shaped by cultural background and personal experiences.[28] In particular, the strong valuing of independence in the United States emphasizes the importance of personal agency and self-determination. This is not necessarily the case in non-Western cultures.[29] Beyond varying cultural interpretations of agency, a wide range of cultural traditions, values, and expectations can play a constraining or enabling role to the development of agency. Young people's experiences are always embedded within larger societal, economic, and institutional contexts (see Figure 3), which influence how they perceive the opportunities and obstacles posed by their environment.[30] Many young people in the United States face significant, very real challenges to developing agency because of a range of factors stemming from these broader structures and contexts; for example, exposure to violence and high levels of stress, or limited access to experiences and opportunities that allow children and adolescents to explore, learn, and try on different roles and identities.[31] This means that for adults working with young people—many of whom are facing obstacles to developing agency—being intentional about the development of agency takes on greater significance in helping youth reach their maximum potential as young adults.

FIGURE 3

Development Occurs Within and Is Influenced by Various Settings and Contexts

26 Rotter (1990).
27 Berlin (1969, p. 131) cited in Moshman (2005, p. 92).
28 Heron (2008); Markus & Kitayama (1991).
29 Hernandez & Iyengar (2001). Agency can have a different focus in different cultures. In cultures that stress interdependence, people tend to define agency in terms of their relationships and perceive their behavior as being contingent on others.
30 Bronfenbrenner (1979); Markus & Kitayama (1991).
31 Emirbayer & Mische (1998).

Psychologist Albert Bandura expands our understanding of agency by defining four things it is comprised of: (1) intentionality that includes having an action plan and strategies for realizing it; (2) forethought to set goals and anticipate likely outcomes in order to guide and motivate actions; (3) self-reactiveness so that one has the self-regulation, skills, and knowledge to carry out a course of action; and (4) self-reflectiveness so that individuals are able to reflect on their personal efficacy, examine the effectiveness and meaning of a course of action, and make adjustments if necessary.[32] Agency thus depends on a range of self-regulatory processes (awareness of the self, metacognition, self-control) as well as knowledge and skills across multiple domains, mindsets such as self-efficacy, and a set of values to guide decision-making. Each of these is included as foundational components in the Foundations for Young Adult Success developmental framework, described in more detail later in this chapter. Agency also depends on having a set of competencies that allow one to navigate and make informed choices in a complex world, a concept we explore below. Finally, agency is aided by having a strong sense of identity across time and multiple social identities. We turn to this idea next.

Integrated Identity

The process of coming to know oneself starts early in life and continues throughout adulthood. Figuring out who one is and developing one's identity is a process of internally integrating various aspects of the self (e.g., beliefs, values, goals, roles, experiences) to create a stable and consistent sense of one's *"wholeness."* This integration process aims toward a sense of continuity with what one has experienced in the past and future possibilities for who one may grow to be.[33] The most active years for identity development fall during adolescence and the transition into young adulthood.[34] Erik Erikson, a developmental psychologist and psychoanalyst who developed one of the most widely applied theories of child and adolescent personality development, described identity formation in adolescence and commitment to an identity in young adulthood as central tasks of development. It is the process of an individual linking childhood with adulthood in a way that situates choice and agency within the individual.[35] Ultimately, a person with a strong identity is able to commit to all facets of the self. Identity, then, is *"not just an attempt to* describe *one's typical behavior; an identity is an account of the core beliefs and purposes that one construes as* explaining *that behavior."* [36]

There is much disagreement among identity theorists as to whether identity formation is a process of discovery, construction, or creation. That is, to what extent is there is a true, innate self to be discovered vs. identity being forged from external forces of environment, experience, and culture vs. the extent to which we actively create our own identities through conscious action and interpretation.[37] A reasonable read of the literature is that it is some of each, and we see this process unfolding through the stages of adolescence and young adulthood, when identity is both a matter of determining who one is and a matter of deciding who one will be.

Much about the formation of identity appears to have changed over the last several decades, as the available options for the person one will become have increased significantly. Historically, youth transitioned directly from adolescence into full adulthood as a function of how society was organized, reaching milestones such as entrance to the full-time workforce and entrance into marriage and starting a family by one's early 20s. As described by James Côté, a sociologist who studies identity formation, young people were expected to enter ready-made roles in adult society; the transition to adulthood was highly normatively structured by gender roles, religious beliefs, and socioeconomic status.[38] Career pathways were more defined and decisions about and the timing of marriage and childbearing were more

---

32 Bandura (2006).
33 McAdams and Adler (2010) refer to this as a narrative identity or authorship.
34 In this paper, we use the term *"young adulthood"* to refer to young people in the transitional *"post-secondary"* period, roughly ages 19 to 22—while acknowledging that, for many, adulthood is still emerging at this age.

35 Erikson (1950/1963, 1968).
36 Moshman (2005, p. 86).
37 Moshman (2005).
38 Côté (1996); Schwartz, Côté, & Arnett (2005).

constrained than they currently are. Thus, previously, the identity challenge for young adults was to find ways to adapt to fixed roles. However, changes in Western industrialized societies have delayed young people's entrance into many of the markers of adulthood that helped to define the self. Researchers studying this new phase of *"emerging adulthood"* (from the late teens into the 20s) have argued that the delay into adulthood has led to greater role ambiguity.[39] In the absence of clear adult roles and social guidelines, making choices about relationships, education, work, values, and commitments is now viewed as a set of individual decisions rather than expected progressions into pre-defined adult roles.[40] This ambiguity surrounding the transition to adulthood adds to the difficulty young people experience in developing a coherent and stable identity.

Adult identity has multiple antecedents across time and context. Children and youth develop many *"selves"* as they grow. They may take on different behaviors, linguistic styles, interests, styles of dress, and even sets of values and self-perceptions in different settings. This is a very normal and important part of growing up. Background characteristics such as race/ethnicity, sexual orientation, gender, and social class also are critical dimensions of identity formation, particularly for young people from marginalized communities.[41] Eventually, however, these different selves can become reconciled into a more coherent identity.

We refer to this process as developing an **integrated identity**—that is, having a sense of internal consistency of who one is across time, across place, and across multiple social realms. An integrated identity provides an internal framework for making sense of how one's choices and actions are related to one's past, one's current social identities, and one's desired future. An integrated identity provides a stable base from which a young person can act in the world. If adolescents *"do not form a coherent sense of self and values, they will lack a consistent sense of identity as they progress into*

adulthood," [42] making the task of navigating multiple contexts particularly complex. Identity development is a lifelong process, but the transition to adulthood is a critical juncture that positions young people for their future; being able to draw one's various strengths and experiences into a more integrated sense of self helps focus skills and efforts more effectively toward setting clear goals, pursuing opportunities, and achieving aims that one sets. As young people are entering into new environments and settings, an integrated identity helps to make this transition more successfully.

Addressing conflicts that may exist between various identities can be a critical struggle for youth throughout adolescence and young adulthood. Context plays a critical role through every stage of this story.[43] In some cases, the contexts in which youth live may vary from the contexts in which they strive to succeed.[44] While developing an integrated identity is a complex process for anyone, for young people growing up in marginalized communities, the task of reconciling different aspects of the self across multiple contexts may be particularly challenging. For example, a youth can have a well-developed identity and set of competencies to navigate difficult terrain with peers in the neighborhood (for example, acting tough or avoiding eye contact), but those strategies may be in direct conflict with expectations in the workplace. One youth profiled in this project, Jermaine, a 20-year-old senior at an alternative high school, has struggled to keep a job because of conflicts with supervisors (**see box** *Youth Profile: Jermaine* **on p.24**). Being a worker under someone else's rules did not fit with the identity he had developed on the streets. Through an experience at a local community center, he began to forge an alternative identity. He has been playing the drums for pay at local churches for years, but until recently this was not something he shared with peers. His mentor at this community center invited him to play at a spoken word poetry event, and he found himself thriving when interacting with kids his age who shared his artistic talents.

23

---

39 Arnett (2000, 2007).
40 Arnett (2000); Mayseless & Keren (2014).
41 Côté (2009); Phillips & Pittman (2003); Phinney (1989); Phinney & Rosenthal (1992).
42 Hazen, Scholzman, & Beresin (2008, p. 163).
43 Bronfenbrenner (1977, 1979, 1986).
44 Patton (2012).

Jermaine

Jermaine, 20, has been kicked out of three Chicago public high schools for fighting. The most recent time was a year ago when another youth came up behind him in the lunchroom.

24

"He balled up his face and got too close," Jermaine recalls. *"I felt threatened."* Jermaine hit him, explaining that if he hadn't, the other guy would have got him first. *"If you don't do it, then they will get you. That's how the streets go."*

Now a senior at an alternative school, he is trying to turn his life around. Seeing some of his friends and relatives head off to college made him want to go, too. So he began doing his homework, going to class, and raising his hand to ask for help when he needed it. Where his prior grades were Cs and Ds, in the fall semester of his senior year he earned a 4.0.

Unfortunately, he is undermining his school success by using strategies for handling conflict with authority figures similar to those he uses to maintain his safety and status on the streets.

For instance, when a teacher recently reprimanded him for talking in class, he cursed her out. *"I'm older now, so I don't take the disrespect,"* he explained. *"If you disrespect me, I'm going to disrespect you back."*

Jermaine, a tall, African American youth, can be disarmingly polite, even charming, when he chooses. But a mentor at the community center in the housing development where Jermaine lives observes, *"Like most teenagers that I run across, Jermaine looks at any form of authority initially as a threat to his manhood or to his* perception of what being a man is. So a lot of time when he is in new situations, he rebels."

That attitude toward authority has gotten him fired from two of the three jobs he's held so far. In one, a summer grounds-keeping job at his housing development, the crew was directed to climb ladders and clean gutters. Jermaine objected to the strenuous work in the hot weather, especially since he hadn't dressed for it that day. He seems to have interpreted the directions to perform the unwanted task as an attempt to dominate him. *"I was like, 'I'm not you-all slave.'"*

Jermaine has at least one aspect of his identity that he keeps separate from his street persona. Since the age of five, he's played the drums and now performs at local church services for pay. *"He's the type of guy [that] would never want any of the other guys from the neighborhood to know he goes to church,"* his mentor notes, *"let alone plays the drums at church."*

His mentor recently invited him to a spoken word poetry event organized by two community youth groups. *"Can I bring my drums? Can I play?"* Jermaine wanted to know. As his mentor explained, the experience of performing with his peers *"made it easier for him to say 'this is what I do.' He is coming into his own identity and being comfortable with it."*

Competencies

The third key factor for young adult success is competencies. **Competencies** are abilities that enable people to successfully perform roles, complete complex tasks, or achieve specific objectives. Young adults require sets of competencies in order to be productive and effective in different settings and adapt to various demands. The last decade has seen an abundance of literature, models, and frameworks (e.g., CASEL, Four Keys for College and Career Success, 4C's) identifying sets of core competencies that are crucial for adolescents transitioning into their young adult lives.[45] Since the start of the new millennium, scholars, youth advocates, and others have been calling attention to the skills demanded by the globalized economy in the 21st century, emphasizing that youth need a broader set of K-12 learning outcomes than content knowledge. Others have noted the need for schools and other youth-serving institutions and programs to develop social-emotional competencies[46] or creativity and innovation[47] as a complement to academic knowledge and skills. There is much evidence to support these calls. Interpersonal skills have been associated with positive academic and developmental outcomes, as seen in the literature on high school engagement[48] and on cooperative studying and student integration in college.[49] Collaboration and positive communication are also highly valued in the workplace, as employers consistently state that communication is one of the most valued traits in workers.[50] Other types of behaviors, such as help-seeking, taking initiative, and getting involved in activities, can also play crucial roles in supporting youth's attainment of their goals.[51]

Across the myriad frameworks identifying the competencies youth need for a successful transition into college or the workplace, there is a great deal of overlap conceptually (even if the terminology is not always consistent). And while some competencies vary across educational, professional, and personal arenas, others are similarly valued across settings.[52] Depending on the paths a young adult chooses to pursue, different competencies will have different saliency, though many such competencies (e.g., the ability to communicate, interact, and think critically) are likely to be necessary for most everyone.

What is the difference between competencies and skills? In the current report, we distinguish these in the following way: Skills refer to the discrete, learned ability to carry out a task with pre-determined results or goals. Competencies, on the other hand, are the abilities to adapt and enact skills in an applied way while drawing on foundational components (self-regulation, knowledge, mindsets, and values) to carry out a task. For example, under our definition, being able to write is a skill. However, being able to write a persuasive letter to the editor about a contentious issue is a competency—it draws on knowledge about the topic, an understanding of one's values and the message one wants to convey, an awareness of the audience, and a belief that one can persuade others. It requires organizing these various components in a particular combination and applying them to meet the demands of a specific task for a specific purpose, making it a competency rather than a skill.

While existing frameworks have value for identifying particular competencies necessary for various settings, they largely overlook the set of foundational components that these competencies rely upon. This is an important gap, as these underlying skills and beliefs need to be attended to and recognized for their critical role in youth development. To take one example, the Partnership for 21st Century Skills created an influential framework focused on the competencies needed to engage in a post-industrial knowledge economy, centering on the 4C's: Communication, Collaboration, Critical Thinking, and Creativity.[53] The term *"21st century skills"* has indeed become shorthand for what young people need in order to succeed in today's world and serves as new end goals in education and youth development. What the 4C's framework does not describe, however, is what underlies and enables these competencies.

45 The Collaborative for Building After-School Systems (2013); Conley (2014); Hewlett Foundation (2013); MHA Labs (2014); Pellegrino & Hilton (2012); Partnership for 21st Century Skills (2009); Savitz-Romer & Bouffard (2012); Weissberg & Cascarino (2013).
46 Weissberg & Cascarino (2013).
47 Wagner & Compton (2012).
48 Fredricks, Blumenfeld, & Paris (2004); Pellegrino & Hilton (2012).
49 Astin (1993); Tinto (1997).
50 Pritchard (2013); International Youth Foundation (2013); Casner & Barrington (2006).
51 Conley (2012).
52 Lippman, Atziena, Rivers, & Keith (2008).
53 Partnership for 21st Century Skills (2009).

The many available frameworks and models that focus on core competencies for college and career often skip over the basic foundational components introduced in this report—components that will be described in detail in the next section. This represents a major distinction between the Foundations for Young Adult Success developmental framework and other frameworks; our focus is on the basic ingredients other competencies depend upon. For example, collaboration—one of the 4C's—consists of working with others effectively and respectfully toward a common goal. Being able to interact with others in a productive manner requires social awareness to be able to read and interpret social cues, strategies to communicate appropriately, and the ability to self-regulate in order to collaborate despite possibly disagreeing with others' viewpoints. Collaboration requires both the flexibility to make compromises as well as the ability to share responsibility for tasks and recognize the value of others' contributions. In these respects, collaboration builds upon a set of skills around working with others, but also requires particular mindsets—such as openness—that allow for an acceptance of ideas that are not self-generated and a valuing of others' contributions. The 4C's heavily rely on knowledge, mindsets, and self-regulation for skills to be implemented appropriately and effectively—all of which are articulated as foundational components in our framework.

The remainder of this chapter expands upon these foundational components that underlie a range of competencies. The Foundations for Young Adult Success developmental framework can be used in conjunction with other existing frameworks to help practitioners better understand not only the higher-level competencies necessary for success, but also the foundational skills and beliefs that are critical to supporting growth and learning in children and youth over the first two decades of life.

Foundational Components

As described above, what lies at the core of the Foundations for Young Adult Success developmental framework is the task of helping youth develop agency, an integrated identity, and competencies that allow a young adult to navigate across multiple contexts in life. Acting with agency requires competencies to manage one's environment, as well as the mindset that this is possible. Building an integrated identity positions young adults for success and supports the utilization of their knowledge and skills toward their tangible goals that reflect their values. All three key factors rely on the strong development of four foundational components described here: self-regulation, knowledge and skills, mindsets, and values.

These foundational components were derived from an extensive review of literature and ongoing conversations with researchers and practitioners from a range of fields. The focus was on both cognitive and noncognitive factors; as pointed out in the earlier UChicago CCSR report, *Teaching Adolescents to Become Learners*,[54] the division between cognitive and noncognitive is extremely fluid, and each category of factors is dependent on the other.[55] For example, being able to collaborate with co-workers to plan an effective meeting is considered a *"noncognitive"* competency, but it relies on a range of factors from having the social skills to get along with others in the planning process and the knowledge of the culture of one's co-workers and workplace (*"cognitive"* capacities).

In addition, the foundational components were chosen because they are malleable. In other words, the foundational components in this framework can be changed by experiences and the efforts of and interactions with other people, in both positive and negative ways and then be internalized. This attention to malleability was

---

54 Farrington et al. (2012).

55 The Foundations for Young Adult Success developmental framework similarly aligns with UChicago CCSR's Noncognitive Framework for Academic Success (Farrington et al., 2012). The 2012 report focuses on foundational skills and beliefs that are critical to supporting growth and learning in the classroom setting. The new framework presented in this report shows how the noncognitive factors highlighted in 2012 fit into a broader set of factors and a broader definition of success. This broader Foundations for Young Adult Success developmental framework also provides more detailed guidance on how adults and contexts can support youth in achieving their goals.

intentional; ultimately, the goal of this work is to help practitioners, parents, program leaders, and other adults who work with children better understand how they can best support development. The process of being changed by experiences and interactions, and internalizing them is core to identity development. We excluded factors such as temperament that, while influential on children's experiences and identity development, are believed to be biologically based and relatively stable over time.[56]

By clearly defining the malleable foundational components that underlie agency, an integrated identity, and competencies, the current framework is intended to be used in conjunction with other work focused on social-emotional learning, deeper learning competencies, noncognitive factors, and 21st century skills. The foundational components are developed and expressed in multiple spheres—within the self, in relation to others, and in the broader world(s) one inhabits.[57] The definitions of each are provided in **Table 1** as a quick reference. We also describe how each foundational component supports the key factors for success, and present evidence of the links between each component and later outcomes in young adulthood. Each foundational component enhances a young person's ability to perceive experiences in ways that encourage positive meaning-making and hence learning.

Self-Regulation

Self-regulation is a set of internal processes that enable one to manage one's own behavior, emotions, attention, and cognition while engaging with the world toward a goal. One comprehensive definition in the literature describes self-regulation as *"the ability to flexibly activate, monitor, inhibit, persevere, and/or adapt one's behavior, attention, emotions, and cognitive strategies in response to direction from internal cues, environmental stimuli, and feedback from others, in an attempt to attain personally*

relevant goals."[58] For young adults, this means being aware of oneself and one's surroundings and managing one's own emotions and behaviors in ways that help move a young person closer to her goals. Various forms of self-regulation include cognitive (including attentional), emotional, social, behavioral, and physiological regulation.[59] There is a growing consensus that these various forms of self-regulation are central to adaptive development[60]—development that allows for adjustment as one proceeds through life—and necessary for both social and cognitive success.[61] Self-regulation allows a person to manage his focus toward an objective, a core part of being able to act with agency.[62] Because of the central role self-regulation plays in almost everything a person does, it not only underlies agency but also supports the ability to develop competencies that can be applied to various settings. Achieving any goal a person sets for himself, successfully interacting with others, and ultimately being able to manage the integration of multiple selves involves self-regulatory processes.

The process of self-regulation requires a multitude of skills; some are more physiological or cognitive in nature (requiring the development of particular areas of the brain), while others are more intentional. Literature suggests that there are two aspects of self-regulation that support successful interactions with others and the world: *self-control*, which is cognitively controlled by executive function (EF) skills, and *awareness*—of oneself, other people, and one's surroundings.

Elements of Self-Regulation
Self-control and the role of executive function skills.
Self-regulatory processes *"include the ability to delay gratification, control impulses, pay attention, and stay on task."*[63] In particular, a set of cognitive functions called EF skills—attentional control, response inhibition,

56 Although these are not things that adults directly change easily, this does not mean that adults should not attend to these traits and consider them as they interact with youth. While temperament is biologically based—something you are born with, rather than something that develops over time—some aspects of temperament are more apt to interact with environments to lead to personality traits (Chess & Thomas, 1977; Goldsmith et al., 1987).
57 The notion that positive youth development requires skills in both the interpersonal (or social) and intrapersonal (or self)

domains has been put forth by other models and frameworks of skills necessary for success in the 21st century (e.g., Pellegrino & Hilton, 2012; Weissberg & Cascarino, 2013).
58 Moilanen (2007, p. 835).
59 See Bronson (2000) for a review.
60 Morrison, Ponitz, & McClelland (2010).
61 Flavell (1979); National Research Council and Institute of Medicine (2000).
62 Zimmerman & Cleary (2006).
63 The Committee for Children (2011).

Chapter 1 | What are the Ingredients of "Success"?

TABLE 1

Definitions of Key Factors and Foundational Components of Young Adult Success

Key Factors		
These three factors support a successful transition into young adulthood and capture how one interacts with the world, sees and understands oneself, and is able to apply one's capabilities to effect change.		
Agency is the ability to make choices about and take an active role in one's life path, rather than solely being the product of one's circumstances. Agency requires the intentionality and forethought to derive a course of action and adjust course as needed to reflect one's identity, competencies, knowledge and skills, mindsets, and values.	**Integrated Identity** is a sense of internal consistency of who one is across time and across multiple social identities (e.g., race/ethnicity, profession, culture, gender, religion). An integrated identity serves as an internal framework for making choices and provides a stable base from which one can act in the world.	**Competencies** are the abilities that enable people to effectively perform roles, complete complex tasks, or achieve specific objectives. Successful young adults have sets of competencies (e.g., critical thinking, responsible decision-making, collaboration) that allow them to be productive and engaged, navigate across contexts, perform effectively in different settings, and adapt to different task and setting demands.

Foundational Components			
These are a set of cognitive and noncognitive components that underlie the three key factors. Each of the four components directly fosters learning and growth, while also reinforcing and enhancing the other foundational components. Each component and subcomponent has corollaries that apply to self, others, or the world.			
Self-Regulation is a set of internal processes that enable one to manage one's behavior, emotions, attention, and cognition while engaging with the world toward a goal. Self-regulation has numerous forms, including cognitive, emotional, behavioral, and attentional regulation. Literature suggests that there are two aspects of self-regulation that support successful interactions with others and the world: *self-control*, which is cognitively controlled by executive function skills, and *awareness*—of oneself, other people, and one's surroundings.	**Knowledge** is sets of facts, information, or understanding about oneself, others, and the world. **Skills** are the learned abilities to carry out a task with intended results or goals. Skills can be general or domain specific, and can be academic, technical, professional, cultural, or institutional in nature. **Knowledge and Skills** are developed over a lifetime, and individuals draw on them in everyday experiences, which help sustain other foundational components and build key factors.	**Mindsets** are beliefs and attitudes about oneself, the external world, and the interaction between the two. They are the default lenses that individuals use to process everyday experiences. Mindsets reflect a person's unconscious biases, natural tendencies, and past experiences. Though mindsets are malleable, they tend to persist until disrupted and replaced with a different belief or attitude.	**Values** are ideals or beliefs about what is good or bad and what is desirable or undesirable. They are important, enduring, and often culturally defined. Values develop through a process of exploration and experimentation, where young people make sense of their experiences and refine what they hold as important ideals. Values serve as broad guidelines for roles and relationships, and provide an orientation for one's desired future.

cognitive flexibility, and working memory—are important for all types of self-regulation.[64] In fact, self-regulation can be thought of as the enactment of EF skills through behaviors.[65] Take, for example, two young men in a verbal disagreement. In an effort to end the disagreement, it takes a great amount of emotional and behavioral regulation for one of those young men to hold back from responding in an angry way. As observers, we are able to see self-regulation play out through his (restrained) behaviors. But what underlies his ability to enact those behaviors is his self-control—the cognitive ability to suppress his natural response, in this case, the strong desire to continue arguing with someone. In the moment, he is capitalizing on his

---

[64] Jones & Bailey (2012); Ponitz, McClelland, Matthews, & Morrison (2009).

[65] Howse, Calkins, Anastopoulos, Keane, & Shelton (2003).

underlying executive function skills—his ability to inhibit automatic responses and think flexibly about ways to improve the situation at hand. Without strong EF skills, it is nearly impossible to self-regulate, leading to a host of struggles for children, adolescents, or adults trying to develop agency, integrated identity, or competencies.

Awareness. Awareness is the conscious focusing of attention. Awareness can be directed toward different objects, resulting in a greater understanding of oneself, one's interactions with others, and one's environment. Awareness is the first step in the ability to self-regulate; to conduct appropriate, positive, and productive behaviors; and ultimately to help bridge the gap between identity building and goal completion. In situations where a young person is intentionally working toward a goal, self-regulation requires *self-awareness* so that she can self-monitor and constantly reassess where she is in relation to that goal.[66] Not only does self-regulation require that we focus our attention on some aspect of either ourselves or our environment, but it also requires *reflecting* on what we are attending to. The absence of reflection results in lost opportunities to understand one's experiences and integrate them into a larger (meta) understanding of oneself in multiple contexts—a topic that is discussed in greater detail in Chapter 2. In these ways, developing the ability to objectively attend to one's actions and reflect on them supports agency; it gives people the insight to adapt their efforts and ultimately achieve their goals.

Metacognition is one specific type of self-awareness that seems to be particularly critical for academic success. Metacognition consists of the ability to be aware of or control one's thinking and understanding so that one can develop strategies to direct thinking toward appropriate goals.[67] For example, a high school student who is studying for a test needs to be able to monitor her level of understanding to know when she has studied enough, or to recognize which parts of the material she needs to spend more time with.

In social contexts, self-regulation requires being *aware of others* (other people and their emotions, other settings/contexts and their social rules); this awareness helps individuals determine appropriate behaviors for the particular social situation they are in (e.g., being empathetic toward someone who is struggling), and supporting the ongoing development of interpersonal competencies. As a person takes stock of his actions and the influence they have on others, it also helps him to consider the type of person he is—both in specific situations and more globally—feeding into an ongoing development of identity. Self-regulation, as a process, is key to identity development among young people because it forms a critical link between thinking about oneself and one's goals and preferences, thinking about one's interaction with others, seeking out and reflecting on feedback, and making choices about one's current and future behavior.

Self-Regulation and Its Relationship to Young Adult Outcomes

It is important to note that in the literature and in existing frameworks, there are many terms used interchangeably with *"self-regulation."* Some refer to constructs similar to the ones described above (e.g., *"emotional competency,"* which includes awareness and identification of one's own emotions[68]), some refer to cognitive capabilities that underlie self-regulation (e.g., executive function abilities such as inhibitory control), and still others combine our notion of self-regulation with other skills and dispositions (e.g., *"self-management"*).[69] Regardless of the various terms used, there is evidence that better self-regulation skills are related to a host of learning and development outcomes from early childhood through young adulthood.

In UChicago CCSR's earlier monograph, *Teaching Adolescents to Become Learners,* the authors noted that in adolescence, self-regulated learners *"monitor the process of their learning, ascertain how effectively they are addressing a given learning task, and adjust their efforts accordingly."*[70] For these older students, self-regulated learning is a goal-oriented process in which adolescents focus awareness on their understanding and select strategies and environments that promote their learning.[71] Indeed, researchers find that

---

66 Gestsdottir & Lerner (2008).
67 Flavell (1979); Hacker, Dunlosky, & Graesser (2009).
68 Philliber Research Associates (2013).

69 Gottfredson & Hirschi (1990); Moroney, Newman, Smith, McGovern, & Yohalem (2014).
70 Farrington et al. (2012, p. 39).
71 Zimmerman (2002).

students of all ages who are more self-regulated display more positive academic outcomes, including grade promotion, higher test scores, and better course grades.[72]

Self-regulation is also related to many social and behavioral outcomes. In one study, college students who had higher levels of self-control (defined by the researchers as a key aspect of self-regulation) exhibited or indicated fewer problems with impulse control, more secure (*"good and stable"*) relationships, better perspective-taking or empathy, and more constructive responses to anger.[73] In other research, those with higher levels of self-control reported being in more satisfying relationships, exhibited lower levels of juvenile delinquency and alcohol abuse, and were more successful supervisors in their jobs.[74]

Most of the current evidence has established *correlations* and *not causality* between self-regulation skills and outcomes. In other words, it has been demonstrated that self-regulation is related to these outcomes (e.g., more self-regulation coincides with better outcomes), but it is not known whether young people's ability to self-regulate actually causes these better outcomes. However, there is early evidence that interventions focusing on self-regulation with adolescents do lead to decreases in violence and crime and increases in academic outcomes.[75] This emerging evidence has important implications for practice. Regardless of the direction of causality, if intentional practices that influence self-regulation also lead to changes in outcomes that matter for youth success, this should be an area of focus for interventions and ongoing supports for youth.

Knowledge and Skills

The role of knowledge and skills for success in young adulthood is commonly recognized. Different types of knowledge and skills play a central role in many of the influential frameworks of core competencies that have emerged in recent years.[76] Broadly speaking, knowledge is the possession of a certain set of facts, information, or understanding. Skills can be defined as having the learned ability to carry out a task with pre-determined results or goals, which can be general or domain-specific. Most of the knowledge and skills that someone has—those that relate to oneself and to interacting with others—are more transferable across contexts; once you have them, you are likely to adapt them to new settings. Knowledge and skills that are related to a person's interaction with *"the world"* are often more specific to a given setting (e.g., having the skill to operate a fork lift).

Academic content and skills are the most obvious set, as they are the primary focus of education in the United States.[77] Indeed, they also are one basis for higher-order competencies that are required for the types of jobs available in the 21st century (for example, science knowledge or computer skills in STEM fields). However, there are a range of other types of knowledge and skills that are crucial for supporting success in young adulthood, yet are generally not an explicit part of formal education. For example, as youth are preparing to enter into the variety of new and different settings that come with the entrance to adulthood, having an understanding of various cultures, contexts, and institutions becomes critical. This includes gaining institutional knowledge—an understanding of how institutions such as universities, workplaces, or communities function and what the norms are for participating in those institutions. Specific institutional knowledge may include knowledge of how to dress appropriately (e.g., a suit for a business job) or of the set of expectations for behavior (e.g., not showing up late for a work meeting), which often vary across different institutions. This type of knowledge and skills are essential to navigate across institutions and allow young adults to act with agency to successfully overcome obstacles and accomplish goals within those institutions.[78]

All children learn the knowledge and skills needed to navigate their cultural environments. However, because institutional knowledge and skills tend to mirror the

---

72 Agostin & Bane (1997); McClelland, Cameron, Connor, Farris, Jewkes, & Morrison (2007); Mischel, Shoda, & Peake (1988); Raver & Knitze (2002); Shoda, Mischel, & Peake (1990); Tangney, Baumeister, & Boone (2004).

73 Tangney, Baumeister, & Boon (2004).

74 Fitzsimons & Finkel (2011).

75 University of Chicago Crime Lab (2012).

76 Conley (2012); MHA Labs (2014); National Center for O*NET Development (2014); Partnership for 21st Century Skills (2009); Pellegrino & Hilton (2012); Weissberg & Cascarino (2013).

77 For example, see the Common Core State Standards (National Governors' Association and Council of Chief State School Officers, 2010).

78 Stanton-Salazar (2011).

cultural norms of the dominant culture, this poses an additional set of skills and knowledge that low-income and minority youth need to learn in order to more easily navigate schools, workplaces, and other institutions. People from low-income and minority backgrounds are often expected to *"code-switch"* so that their behaviors match the norms of a given institution (e.g., a college classroom), rather than their own cultural norms. This requires having an additional set of knowledge and skills, as well as other foundational components such as self-regulation.

Interpersonal knowledge and skills represent another important subset of this foundational component. Interpersonal knowledge is specific to knowing the norms for interacting with other people in a given setting or from a particular culture. Having the skills to implement this well is evidenced by the ability to act according to those norms. For example, interpersonal knowledge may help a person to understand the appropriate topics to raise with work colleagues versus close friends, and interpersonal skills allow a person to enact those rules in the applicable situations. Often, enacting interpersonal skills according to social rules also relies on emotional or behavioral self-regulation—an example of how the foundational components support each other while also underlying the key factors for success and later young adult outcomes.

Knowledge and skills and their relationship to young adult outcomes. A 2012 National Research Council (NRC) report argued that there are three domains of knowledge, skills, and dispositions that are necessary for success in education, work, and other areas of adult responsibility: the cognitive domain (cognitive processes and strategies, creativity, and knowledge), the intrapersonal domain (intellectual openness, work ethic and conscientiousness, and positive core self-evaluation), and the interpersonal domain (teamwork and collaboration and leadership).[79] In their report,

the NRC committee provided an overview of the existing literature on the links between all of these types of knowledge and skills and more successful outcomes for young adults. As with self-regulation, they note that most of the evidence is correlational rather than causal. Nonetheless, there is ample correlational evidence that academic achievement is related to a host of positive outcomes. The NRC committee found that there are modest associations between early achievement (related to knowledge) and later outcomes; interestingly, the strongest relationships exist when looking at youth who have *"persistent deficits"* in their knowledge and skills. Those with achievement deficits have a much lower likelihood of graduating from high school and attending college than those without achievement deficits.[80]

The NRC committee also found that greater levels of knowledge and skills are related to outcomes once out of school. Investments in education (which primarily focus on the acquisition of content knowledge and skills) produce the largest returns through higher levels of income. The more years a person is in school, the greater the benefits and satisfaction a person receives through her job. It is important to note that some research suggests that this relationship occurs because of better ongoing educational opportunities that are afforded to higher-scoring students, and is not due to a direct link between knowledge and income. Nonetheless, greater acquisition of knowledge and skills begets better opportunities for an individual over time, regardless of socioeconomic status.[81]

Mindsets

Mindsets are psycho-social beliefs and attitudes about oneself, the external world, and the interaction between the two. Mindsets are the brain's way of efficiently organizing our interpretation of the world. They are the default lenses we use to process everyday experience. Mindsets are malleable, but unless something challenges them—or challenges a conclusion we arrived

---

79 Pellegrino & Hilton (2012).
80 Duncan & Magnuson (2011).
81 Currie & Thomas (1999).

at because of them—we will continue to use these interpretive lenses as a shortcut method of attributing motives, construing cause and effect, interpreting how we fit in, anticipating likely consequences, and approaching new experiences, among other things. Mindsets are mutually reinforced by one's knowledge and awareness, as people use what they already think to make sense of new experience. As one recognizes and interprets new experiences and information through one's default mindsets, this new, interpreted knowledge in turn *"justifies"* the existing mindsets. In essence, people see what they are looking for. Mindsets also interact with self-regulation by coloring one's awareness, which in turn guides one's selection of strategies and behaviors. It is crucial that in practice, adults attend to the developing mindsets of youth. There is a danger that if positive mindsets are not intentionally supported, negative or otherwise detrimental or maladaptive mindsets may arise. Youth may then be susceptible to ongoing, reinforcing negative interpretations of themselves and the world, ultimately interfering with their achievement of positive outcomes. For illustrative purposes only, we briefly examine three mindsets—self-efficacy, openness, and a growth mindset—to demonstrate how mindsets operate across contexts to support young adult success.[82]

Self-efficacy is the belief that one is able to succeed at a given task.[83] As Bandura wrote, *"Among the mechanisms of agency, none is more central or pervasive than people's beliefs about their capabilities to exercise control over their own level of functioning and over events that affect their lives. Efficacy beliefs influence how people feel, think, motivate themselves, and behave."*[84] Self-efficacy seems to play a particularly important role in supporting the key factor of agency in young adulthood.

The research on self-efficacy consistently finds that individuals are more likely to engage in tasks they feel confident they can successfully complete and to withdraw from tasks for which they lack such confidence.[85] The belief that one will succeed at a task is associated with the level of effort one expends as well as one's likelihood to persist in the face of challenges.[86] Most of the literature agrees that self-efficacy is domain specific and even task specific, meaning that the belief one can succeed is limited to specific cases (e.g., the belief that one can complete a particular set of difficult math problems) rather than being broadly generalized, even within a domain. It is unclear whether self-efficacy might spread over time or *"spill over"* to become a more generalized expectation about one's performance in life. Another open question is how the development or importance of self-efficacy might vary for different subgroups in different contexts. These remain areas in need of further research.[87]

Openness is a broad set of attitudes that encompass an individual's receptiveness to new and unfamiliar ideas, feelings, and experiences as well as interest in new people and places.[88] Though openness is counted as one of the *"Big Five"* personality traits, which are viewed as relatively fixed characteristics of a person, there is a general understanding that openness can be developed through exposure to new experiences, particularly in the context of a secure base from which to venture forth. Individual openness increases over childhood through young adulthood[89] and is associated with a general flexibility in thinking.[90] Openness is more than a passive psychological trait, but rather also includes the motivation and actions to seek out new experiences and the ability to adapt to new experiences, whether or not they have been sought out.[91]

---

82 This list of mindsets differs slightly from the four academic mindsets we reviewed in our earlier report, *Teaching Adolescents to Become Learners* (Farrington et al., 2012). From that earlier list, we could just as easily have included relevance and belonging here, as these mindsets could also provide strong supports for success in young adulthood. Because we have broadened our focus in this report to outcomes beyond academic performance and are considering multiple contexts beyond the classroom (e.g., family, community, out-of-school programs), we add here the mindset of openness, which has evidence of playing a particularly important role in supporting young adult success.

83 Bandura (1986).
84 Bandura (1993, p. 118).
85 Bandura (1986).
86 Bandura & Schunk (1981); Bouffard-Bouchard (1990); Pajares (1996); Schunk & Mullen (2012).
87 Lennon (2010); Schunk & Meece (2006).
88 Dignan (1990); McCrae & Sutin (2009).
89 McCrae et al. (2002).
90 McCrae & Sutin (2009).
91 McCrae & Costa (1997).

A **growth mindset** is the belief that ability and skill are malleable and will increase in response to one's effort rather than being fixed and outside of one's control. Similar to self-efficacy beliefs, having a growth mindset is advantageous because it affects how one interprets and responds to struggle and failure and makes a person more likely to persevere in the face of challenge.[92] People with growth mindsets are more self-motivating and persistent than people with fixed mindsets, and they expend effort to build their competence rather than withdrawing from difficult tasks.[93]

Mindsets are inextricably related to the other foundational pieces of the framework—self-regulation, knowledge and skills, and values. The extent to which individuals are aware of themselves and others and able to harness that awareness to propel themselves forward may be closely associated with their beliefs and attitudes. Likewise, we expect mindsets to be recursively influenced by other aspects of the framework.[94] For example, being able to engage in effective behaviors or to self-regulate may affect one's sense of self-efficacy, openness, and belief in one's ability to grow. Further, maintaining a sense of purpose and a belief that *"I matter"* is only possible if the world one apprehends feels within one's control and responsive to one's actions. Mindsets such as openness, growth, and self-efficacy are likely to support young people in cultivating a larger sense of purpose and taking action to achieve that purpose. Given the roles mindsets play in perseverance, they are also intricately related to agency. Adaptive mindsets can provide the positive beliefs a person needs to go after her ambitions and push through obstacles that may stand in her way.

Mindsets and Their Relationship to Young Adult Outcomes

All three mindsets illustrated here (as well as those reviewed in our 2012 report) have been linked to higher levels of achievement and other outcomes for young adult success. High self-efficacy has been linked to greater commitment to goals, use of more effective strategies, and a better response to negative feedback.[95] As summarized by Lennon (2010), students with high academic self-efficacy set academic goals, commit to those goals, and view problems as challenges to be mastered. When they experience failure or receive critical feedback, they redouble their efforts to improve their performance rather than interpreting failure as diagnostic of their capabilities. Because strong self-efficacy beliefs affect how one construes and responds to setbacks, self-efficacy increases one's likelihood for success, regardless of actual ability level;[96] thus, self-efficacy is an important ingredient for young adult success.

Due to its diffuse and multi-faceted nature, researchers have historically had more difficulty isolating the beneficial effects of openness.[97] Despite these limitations, openness has been associated with a number of important outcomes, including healthy relationships,[98] academic test scores,[99] and job performance.[100] The role of openness (or its mechanism of association) in other psychological or social outcomes has yet to be thoroughly explored. It is possible, for example, that openness might allow individuals to be more flexible in coping with difficult situations, or that being open to and seeking new experiences might allow an individual to take better advantage of resources and opportunities. As will be shown in Chapter 3, openness to a range of new adult roles (rather than prematurely narrowing one's options) seems to have long-term benefits for young adults.

33

---

92 Dweck (1975).
93 Cury, Elliott, Da Fonseca, & Moller (2006);
    Dweck & Leggett (1988).
94 Farrington et al. (2012).
95 Locke & Latham (2002).

96 Farrington et al. (2012).
97 McCrae et al. (2002).
98 McCrae (1996); Ozer & Bennet-Martinez (2006).
99 Noftle & Robbins (2007).
100 Barrick & Mount (1991); Tett, Jackson, & Rothstein (1991).

Growth mindsets have been found to be influential for success in school as well as across a variety of other contexts.[101] Interventions designed to build growth mindsets have tended either to use explicit instruction on neuroplasticity—teaching students that the brain is *"like a muscle"* that gets stronger with use—or to focus on giving process-oriented feedback that emphasizes student effort or strategy use rather than innate ability, e.g., *"You did very well; you must have worked hard on that"* rather than *"You did very well; you must be really smart at this."* Interestingly, even brief, targeted comments such as these can be enough to *"switch off"* a more fixed mindset and *"switch on"* a more growth-oriented mindset, at least temporarily—and experimental studies show that students who receive *"growth-mindset feedback"* tend to perform better than control subjects on subsequent experimental tasks.[102] The belief that hard work pays off seems to have obvious benefits across a variety of domains, beginning most notably in early adolescence when young people begin to differentiate between ability and effort and begin forming a stronger sense of their own competencies.[103]

Although most of the literature focuses on relationships between mindsets and academic outcomes, the extrapolation to other sectors of a person's life is not difficult. Believing that new opportunities are worth pursuing, that one has the capabilities to be successful at something, and that more effort will result in growth are likely to serve a young adult well. Such an adaptive belief can be directed toward one's home life, work life, college life, or other interests.

Values

One of the major influences on how young adults approach their life path and interact with others and the world is based on their *values*, the fourth foundational component of our framework. Values are lasting beliefs, often culturally defined, about what is good or bad and what is important in life, which serve as broad guidelines for living and provide an orientation for the future.[104] Values include both the moral code of conduct one uses in daily activities (e.g., being kind, being truthful) and long-term *"outcomes"* of importance (e.g., getting an education, having the respect of friends, contributing to the community) that may not necessarily have a right or wrong valence.[105] Having a sense of one's values is one of the core components of identity formation and can be used to guide the commitments young adults make to roles, beliefs, and relationships as they try to find a place in the larger society.[106] Values motivate how one engages with the world, whether it is with a specific behavior or something broader such as an occupation or role.

As youth develop, the internalization of experiences and relationships shapes their values, consciously and unconsciously. The development of agency and identity is shaped by whether youth have a clear *sense* of their values, whatever those values are. Being able to articulate those and focus on aligning their efforts with those values helps youth and young adults to go after a set of cohesive goals that align with the person they want to be. Having a sense of values also helps a person distinguish between something that is morally right or wrong, or between something that would have a positive or a negative effect on one's community. As young children mature, there is a realization that morality is not black and white, and one's values tend to provide some shading for those morals.

Values and Their Relationship to Young Adult Outcomes

Values, such as caring about whether something has social value, shape how young adults engage in roles. For example, observational studies of individuals in low-status occupations found that motivation and performance are strongly connected to the perception of that work as having larger social value.[107] Individuals in a wide range of occupations and professional settings, including hospital orderlies, prison guards, telemarket-

101 Dweck (2006).
102 Dweck (2002); Mueller & Dweck (1998).
103 Eccles et al. (1993); Farrington et al. (2012).
104 Braithwaite & Law (1985); Weber (1993).
105 Rokeach (1971) distinguishes between terminal values, which are the end-state goals an individual would like to achieve

during his or her lifetime, and instrumental values, which are the behaviors and code of conduct that can get one there.
106 Hazen, Scholzman, & Beresin (2008).
107 Yeager et al. (2014); see also Ashforth & Kreiner (1999); Dutton, Roberts, & Bednar (2010); Hughes (1958, 1962); Wrzesniewski, Dutton, & Debebe (2003); Olivola & Shafir (2013).

ers,[108] and medical professionals,[109] all demonstrate greater commitment to performing their jobs at a high level when that work is explicitly linked to serving a larger social purpose, such as helping the poor or eliminating disease and improving others' health.[110] One's values and commitments also *provide resources for emerging adults to counteract the anomie and lack of collective support associated with identity formation and the transition to adulthood in the United States.*[111]

Implications

The foundational components include having the self-regulation to plan, manage, and follow through on a given set of actions; knowledge and skills to navigate various situations; positive mindsets about the opportunities available and the ability to capitalize on those opportunities; and a strong sense of values. Together, these make an individual more likely to attain her goals. However, these foundational components do not *directly* lead to young adult success. It is through the development of the foundational components that young adults are able to effectively act with agency, build an integrated identity, and have strong competencies.

Additionally, it is important to note that although the foundational components are depicted here as four separate components, they are intricately interrelated and mutually reinforcing (much like agency, integrated identity, and competencies). By the time an individual reaches adolescence, these components have developed alongside one another *and* influenced the development of each other. Having strength in any one component is likely to strengthen the other components, and deficits in one component can hinder the development of other components. Ultimately, strong connections among these four foundational components make possible a wide range of competencies and processes, including critical thinking, problem-solving, collaborating, responsible decision-making, network-building, constructing an integrated identity that brings together one's past and future, and having the agency to navigate fearlessly through different social worlds. In turn, it is experiences and relationships within a person's social worlds that reciprocally develop these foundational components. It is these very developmental experiences and developmental relationships that we address next.

---

108 Grant (2008).

109 Grant & Hoffman (2011).

110 Feiler, Tost, & Grant (2012); Grant & Rothbard (forthcoming); Sansone, Weir, Harpster, & Morgan (1992).

111 Schwartz, Côté, & Arnett (2005, p. 223).

36

CHAPTER 2

The Importance of Developmental Experiences and Relationships

⟫ Key Points

///

- Developmental experiences are opportunities for *action and reflection* that help young people build self-regulation, knowledge and skills, mindsets, and values, and develop agency, integrated identity, and competencies.

- Developmental experiences are *"maximized"* in the context of social interactions with others.

- Experience must be assigned meaning and be integrated into one's emerging sense of identity if it is to have lasting or transferrable benefit. Mediating young people's thinking about their experience is one important way that adults aid in learning and development.

- When young people have the opportunity to make contributions that are valued by others, they gain self-confidence and come to see themselves as capable and able to effect change in their own lives and in the larger world.

- Strong, supported, and sustained relationships with caring adults provide an important space for youth to experiment, try out roles and behaviors, and receive feedback that helps to shape how they ultimately construct an integrated identity.

- Educators, parents, childcare providers, and youth workers need opportunities and support to develop the knowledge and skills to create meaningful experiences for youth.

- Children's opportunities for development vary significantly by race and socioeconomic class. Providing more equitable opportunities is critical to achieving a just society and realizing the potential of young people in the United States.

///

In the introduction and Chapter 1, we presented a set of key factors (agency, integrated identity, and competencies) and the foundational components that underlie them (self-regulation, knowledge and skills, mindsets, and values) that would be emblematic of a young person who is able to succeed in the educational, economic, social, and civic tasks of young adulthood. We touched briefly upon the way these foundational components and key factors are mutually reinforcing, helping young people to both learn from and proactively shape their worlds. We turn now to the question of *how* these foundational components and key factors can be intentionally developed. How do children learn knowledge, skills, values, mindsets, and the complex processes of self-regulation? How do they develop agency, an integrated identity, and competencies essential to success in the 21st century? In this chapter, we focus on what is known about the transformation of children's daily experience into *learning and becoming.* We explore how

adults might help youth develop a set of navigational tools for exploring the world, an adaptive orientation toward life, and the habitual positive behaviors associated with *"good character."* We begin with a focus on what we are terming **developmental experiences**, drawing from key principles of how youth learn, and then turn to the importance of **developmental relationships** as essential social contexts for these experiences.

Development is a natural, ongoing process as young people observe the world, interact with others, and make meaning of their experiences. Regardless of the degree of adult guidance, children will still *"develop"* in some way, learning how to do things and coming to conclusions about themselves, what they value, their prospects, and their paths forward. They will develop some skills and preferences, and they will likely figure out much they need to know. And yet, the developmental benefit of children's experiences can be enhanced and directed by others to help youth best formulate and internalize the developmental *"lessons"* from these experiences.[112] Participating on a Little League team can simply be the experience of having fun playing baseball (perhaps an important goal in itself), but it can also be a rich opportunity for children to build social skills for interacting with adults and peers, learn to regulate behavior in line with shared rules, visit other communities and gain cultural awareness, develop athletic competencies and habits of physical fitness, learn strategies for dealing with setbacks, or figure out how to do batting practice even when friends want to play video games.

Young people's daily lives are a continual stream of experiences and social interactions; intentional adult practices can alter the nature and substance of these experiences and interactions to guide them toward important developmental goals. As young people grow, adults should give them increasing responsibility for making choices about and ascribing meaning to the experiences and relationships they pursue.

Developmental Experiences

We define developmental experiences as those activities that provide children and youth with the necessary conditions and stimuli to advance their development as appropriate to their age. Developmental experiences provide rich opportunities for youth to build the foundational components of self-regulation, knowledge and skills, mindsets, and values; to practice competencies; and to foster the capabilities to have agency and an integrated identity in young adulthood. As will be clear throughout this chapter, developmental experiences are *"maximized"* in the context of social interactions with others—in strong, supported, and sustained relationships with adults and peers that are set within caring communities. For developmental experiences to have a lasting and transferrable impact, the insights, developing skills, or other lessons generated by these experiences must be integrated into one's larger sense of self in a way that expands a young person's competencies and agency in the world. We describe developmental experiences in full before moving to a discussion of

developmental relationships, but it should be emphasized that, in practice, development flourishes in the context of social relationships and community.

How Humans Learn and Develop

Our understanding of human learning has significantly improved over the past several decades, fueled in part by technological advances that enable much more intricate observations of the human brain at work. Learning is no longer understood as amassing facts in card-catalog fashion, or as trained behavioral responses to stimuli, but rather as changes in the complex neural interconnections in the brain; these neural connections are then *"felt"* as changes in our sense of understanding, or in our subjective experience of ourselves in the world. We focus here on broad lines of work that depict learning as experiential and social, as well as work that examines the underlying neurological components of learning. Though there are still many unanswered questions in the human cognitive sciences, existing research suggests compelling courses of action for adults working with and on behalf of children and youth.

Drawing from research on how children learn and how habits are developed,[113] we offer a model for developmental experiences as including both *active ("building")* and *reflective ("meaning-making")* aspects. As depicted in the Foundations for Young Adult Success developmental framework (see Figure 1), these experiences help strengthen the foundational components and key factors as youth grow up. The active aspects provide opportunities for children and youth to become more sophisticated in their self-regulation and to build knowledge and skills, mindsets, values, and to foster agency, an integrated identity and competencies. Building the foundational components and key factors for success in young adulthood depends on active opportunities to *encounter, tinker, practice, choose,* and *contribute.* Youth cannot build their capacities or develop expertise without these opportunities. However, though these active aspects of developmental experiences are necessary, they are not sufficient for learning.

---

112 Vygotsky (1978).
113 Bransford, Brown, & Cocking (2000); Ericsson & Charness (1994); Lally, Van Jaarsveld, Potts, & Wardle (2010).

Young people also require opportunities to make meaning of their active participation and of the competencies they are building. The reflective aspects of developmental experiences provide opportunities to *describe* one's growing understanding of the world and *evaluate* various aspects of one's performance or one's choices; to *connect* experiences to other things youth know, experience, and care about; and to *envision* possibilities for the future. Over time, a key part of reflective activities is to *integrate* developmental experiences into one's self-concept and the *"story"* of oneself; this is the path to building agency and an integrated identity. Below, we describe in more detail the dual aspects of developmental experiences—acting and reflecting. In Chapter 3, we consider how knowledge of child and adolescent development can be used to best tailor developmental experiences for young people at various developmental stages, from early childhood through young adulthood.

The Action Reflection Cycle

The Active Aspects of Developmental Experiences

A long tradition of work in philosophy, psychology, and education emphasizes the critical role of experience in learning.[114] Educational theorist David Kolb defined learning as *"the process whereby knowledge is created through the transformation of experience."* [115] This kind of direct experience—*"the concrete, tangible, felt qualities of the world, relying on our senses, and immersing ourselves in concrete reality"*—is one of the primary ways children perceive new information and develop an understanding of the world.[116] But certain types of experiences provide richer opportunities for development than others (**see Figure 4**). Generally speaking, children need active opportunities to observe models, to tinker, to practice, to make choices, and ultimately to contribute work of value to others. Rich developmental experiences include those that put children in interaction with peers and adults; build strong and supportive relationships; and provide opportunities to play and explore, try on new roles and perspectives, publicly demonstrate new skills and competencies, and contribute to endeav-

ors that are personally and socially meaningful. Below, we examine each of these experiences further.

Encountering. For children to develop awareness of themselves, others, and the world, they need access to new people, new ideas, new roles, and new places. To develop self-regulation, skills, and competencies, they need clear models of behavior, of skilled performance, and of high-quality products. Many of the practitioners we interviewed for this project emphasized the importance of exposing children to novel things and situations. Crystal Elliott-O'Connor, associate director of early childhood development at Family Focus, emphasized that the educators she worked with were *"really making sure that children have very, very rich and very many experiences…to just play in novel ways, with materials and supplies and equipment that maybe they would not normally get or see outside of the classroom."* [117] Another interviewee, Blair Root, the director of a neighborhood club that serves school-aged children, noted that it is important to offer *"different hands-on learning activities…to introduce [children] to activities they may not have had the opportunity to [try], whether just playing football, doing some science with them, or art, or a fencing program."* [118] For older youth to develop a sense of who

FIGURE 4

Building Foundations for Young Adult Success Through Developmental Experiences

---

114 Dewey (1938); James (1912); Freire (1970/ 1993); Kolb (1984); Mezirow (1985, 2000).
115 Kolb (1984, p. 41).
116 Kolb (1984).

117 UChicago CCSR Interview with Crystal Elliott-O'Connor, Associate Director, Family Focus (September 24, 2014).
118 UChicago CCSR interview with Blair Root, director, Hyde Park Neighborhood Club (October 29, 2014).

they want to be and the kind of work they want to do when they enter adulthood, they need opportunities *"to learn about (and more selectively, to experience) the range of adult roles—the kinds of technical, scientific, artistic, social, and civic tasks that adults devote themselves to, and the range of roles in particular vocational arenas."* [119]

Encountering also means watching others and examining models or exemplars. Many young people engage in *"reflective observation"* as their primary means for taking in information about the world. [120] They carefully watch adults or other youth and incorporate their behaviors, their speech patterns, and their preferences. Young people also look to others to learn new skills and influence their values. Healthy relationships with adults are critical for youth development, as it is from adults that young people learn *"how one listens, thinks, relates to other people, responds, formulates questions, handles conflict, provides feedback, and reconciles differences in perspective."* [121] Vygotsky pointed to the role of *"more capable peers"* and adult guides in demonstrating how to do things children cannot figure out or execute alone. [122] Role models can demonstrate behaviors and language appropriate to a given situation or setting—for example, how to engage with adults in a professional workplace, how to advocate for oneself at a doctor's office, or how to chop logs into firewood. As Halpern, Heckman, and Larson write in their report on adolescent learning, young people learn best when they are immersed in a *"community of practice"* that *"allows its newest members to watch, listen to, and emulate...more experienced members. It provides models of action. It gives less experienced learners opportunity to see all the steps in addressing a problem before they are ready to accomplish these steps independently."* [123]

Encountering models is essential in situations where youth are expected to deliver some kind of performance or create a final product, whether writing a research paper, playing a sonata, preparing a lasagna dinner, or changing the tire on the family car. Without clear

models of what they are working toward (i.e., what it would look, feel, sound, or taste like if it were done well), young people have a difficult time directing their efforts. Seeing both the final product and the process for creating it aids in developing competencies and potential identities. Not only can adults act as role models who demonstrate appropriate behaviors for specific situations, but they can also provide youth with clear examples of quality work. [124] Ron Berger, chief academic officer for the Expeditionary Learning (EL) network of schools, is a particularly strong advocate of the importance of high-quality models. He wrote,

> Models are important in all ways for youth: models of the kinds of work they need to do, but equally models of how to act in different situations, models of what they could become, models of communities they can aspire to join or create. Adults are often telling adolescents what is possible, what they can become, but unless those kids see models of what [that] actually looks like—other young adults or adults who are successful examples—it's hard to have a vision of what they are aiming for or believe it is possible. When new students enter successful EL schools, I think the power of models is what transforms them. Everywhere they look, there is student work on the walls that is a model of the quality of what is expected, there are older students who are taking their academic success seriously, treating others well and showing academic courage, there are adults who are modeling respectful communication and integrity.
> —Ron Berger, chief academic officer, Expeditionary Learning [125]

---

119 Halpern, Heckman, & Larson (2013).
120 Kolb (1984).
121 Halpern, Heckman, & Larson (2013, p. 15).
122 Vygotsky (1978).

123 Halpern, Heckman, & Larson (2013, p. 10).
124 Berger (2003).
125 Ron Berger, chief academic officer, Expeditionary Learning, email communication with the authors (February 2015).

Encountering new ideas, new places, and models of what is possible is one of the most important developmental experiences young people can have.

Tinkering. Providing opportunities for children and youth to actively discover, design, puzzle, build, experiment, create, play, imagine, test, and generally jump in and *do* is essential to their developing knowledge about the physical world and how things work. Participating in activities together also gives young people opportunities to negotiate ideas with others, take on different perspectives, and practice self-regulatory skills (e.g., focusing attention, inhibiting impulses, taking turns). Physical engagement also helps children test (and learn) their limits and challenges them to stretch past the edge of their comfort and existing abilities to expand their capabilities.

Many practitioners emphasized the importance of providing children with rich exploratory opportunities, particularly when we were talking with out-of-school providers or educators working with young children. Vanessa Schwartz, a program supervisor, explained that a goal of the home-visiting and other early childhood programs that she oversees is to *"let the child direct the play, and not have the adult try to direct how a child does things...to help develop that child's creativity and problem-solving skills, instead of being told"* how things should be done.[126] Melinda Berry, senior family support specialist with Educare Chicago, echoed this perspective even for the very youngest of children, noting the importance of balancing safety for infants and toddlers with *"enough freedom to explore and learn on their own."*[127] Providing extended and uninterrupted periods of time for children to explore their environments has been a central tenet of the Montessori approach to education for over a hundred years. Likewise, the now-widespread philosophy of early childhood education developed in Reggio Emilia, Italy, also sees children's exploration and

experimentation as essential for healthy development. Both of these approaches emphasize the creation of richly stimulating environments as settings for children's exploration and imaginative play, and indeed, this is accepted practice in early childhood environments around the country.

Unfortunately, much of the emphasis on play and exploration seems to disappear as soon as children enter formal schooling. As Expeditionary Learning's Ron Berger noted about traditional school transitions, preschoolers and kindergartners get *"play areas and block areas and toys and drama centers and dress up centers. And then the kids go into first grade, and they're just a few months older, where there are just desks in rows, and no way to be active and creative."*[128] There is little opportunity to tinker in formal K-12 settings. This is a mistake, because opportunities to be creative are indispensable to children's learning. In a 21st century economy that prizes creativity and innovation, youth need repeated opportunities to engage in challenging, open-ended tasks that require them to think *"outside of the box"* and grapple with difficult problems. They also need opportunities for imaginative play. UC Berkeley psychology professor Alison Gopnik notes:

> Conventional wisdom suggests that knowledge and imagination, science and fantasy, are deeply different from one another—even opposites. But...the same abilities that let children learn so much about the world also allow them to change the world—to bring new worlds into existence—and to imagine alternative worlds that may never exist at all. Children's brains create causal theories of the world, maps of how the world works. And these theories allow children to envisage new possibilities, and to imagine and pretend that the world is different.[129]

41

126 UChicago CCSR interview with Vanessa Schwartz, program supervisor, Metropolitan Family Services (October 3, 2014).

127 UChicago CCSR interview with Melinda Berry, senior family support specialist, Educare Chicago (September 18, 2014).

128 UChicago CCSR interview with Ron Berger, Chief Academic Officer, Expeditionary Learning (September 19, 2014).

129 Gopnik (2009, p. 21).

Gopnik and her colleagues believe that imaginative play helps prepare children for serious adult activities, such as setting goals, anticipating challenges, and planning for contingencies. They argue that *"counterfactual reasoning,"* the ability to imagine an alternative representation of reality, *"is a crucial tool that children need to plan for the future and learn about the world."* This is a basic component of *"design thinking,"* an approach to creating solutions that is increasingly valued in business, engineering, architecture, urban planning, and education. As design science theorist John Chris Jones wrote, designers *are forever bound to treat as real that which exists only in an imagined future and have to specify ways in which the foreseen thing can be made to exist."* [130] While school may provide fewer opportunities for tinkering and creative play as children get older, young people continue to need exploratory experiences to lay the tracks for handling adult responsibilities[131] and developing competencies for the 21st century.

For older adolescents, tinkering often takes the form of a more grown-up version of early childhood role play. Teenagers try on different personas as a way of test-driving potential adult roles. Older adolescents who are presented with and encouraged to explore a wide variety of opportunities, roles, and life possibilities before prematurely deciding on one course have more agency and are better able to achieve an integrated identity in young adulthood.[132] Continuing to provide opportunities to play, explore, and tinker for children and youth of all ages, across all contexts, strongly supports the development of the foundational components and the key factors of young adult success.

Practicing. While children learn by encountering and tinkering, they also need opportunities to practice in order to build competencies over time. There is strong empirical support for practice as a major factor in developing expertise.[133] However, just doing something repetitively does not lead to improvement.[134] In fact, repeated practice can reinforce bad habits or incorrect approaches if one doesn't have a way to recognize what one is doing wrong. Instead, *"deliberate practice"* emphasizes the importance of motivation, adequate strategies, and accurate feedback, as well as repeated and focused effort over time to push oneself and develop expertise.[135] Comparing one's performance against an explicit outcome or a mental model[136] is an essential component of effective practice. Knowledgeable teachers, coaches, or tutors who observe young people's practice and provide immediate feedback ensure that errors are caught early and corrected before they become engrained. Repeated physical or mental actions established through practice can strengthen neural pathways across the parts of the brain that are engaged in the repeated activity. Advances in neuroscience support the benefits of motivated, deliberate practice—and point to the inextricable connections between emotion and learning. Neuroscientists *"now know that in order for practice to induce learning-dependent brain changes it must be meaningful, motivating, skillful, challenging, and rewarding."* [137]

Practice not only builds expertise over time, but also reinforces motivation for continued learning. Intrinsic motivation develops as youth *"learn more about a topic, experience competence in it, and connect with others who share this interest"* and gain practice applying *"the tools of a discipline in creative and generative ways...[and] make them their own."* [138] As young people practice their skills in a community that values expertise in a given area, they become better able to manage the tedious parts of practice and to sustain their interest in improving their craft.[139] For example, in the popular *"School of Rock"* music schools that have sprung up around the country, children and youth engage in a performance-based approach to learning music that has them almost immediately practicing in a band with their peers. Youth who are experienced musicians play together

130 Jones (1992).
131 Weisberg & Gopnik (2013, p. 1368).
132 Berzonsky (1989); Kroger (1993); Marcia (1966); Savitz-Romer & Bouffard (2012); Schwartz, Côté, & Arnett (2005).
133 Ericsson & Charness (1994).
134 Kolb & Kolb (2009).
135 Ericsson, Krampe, & Tesch-Römer (1993).
136 Keeton, Sheckley, & Griggs (2002).
137 Winstein (2014).
138 Halpern, Heckman, & Larson (2013, p. 12).
139 Hidi & Renninger (2006).

with newcomers as they prepare for a live performance in an established music venue. Ultimately, whether in music, sports, academics, or any number of other endeavors, practice prepares children and youth to be successful in future performances. Opportunities for practice take on particular importance in the teenage years. *"If development is 'rehearsals' for becoming an adult,"* says developmental psychologist Abigail Baird, *"then adolescence is the final 'dress rehearsal' before you have to take the stage, and you need as much experience— with both success and failure—as possible."* [140]

Choosing. As children learn and grow, an important developmental experience involves the opportunity to make choices for themselves. Psychologists have long noted that human beings need to feel in control of their own destiny; many see autonomy as a basic psychological need.[141] But how do young people achieve autonomy in a world that necessarily imposes all kinds of restrictions on their actions? One psychological theory, called self-determination theory, defines *"autonomous acts"* as those that are consciously chosen by a coherent self. This does not imply that autonomous choices are not constrained by outside circumstance, but rather that the human actor recognizes those constraints or influences and makes a conscious choice within them.[142]

At every age, making choices fosters cognitive, moral, and social development.[143] For very young children, choices are likely to be highly structured and posed by adults—*"Would you rather play outside on the swings or stay inside and read books this morning?"*—while older youth often have to figure out for themselves what their options are in a given situation before choosing what to do. For adolescents, choosing may involve complex decision-making about how to act with integrity amidst competing social pressures or how to act morally by weighing conflicting values. Young people need to experience increasing autonomy over their lives in order to

build toward agency in young adulthood. This means being increasingly able to choose their activities, their companions, how they spend their time, the ways they present themselves, and decisions that will affect their future.

The importance of choosing is reflected in the inclusion of *"responsible decision making"* in CASEL's model of social-emotional learning core competencies. CASEL defines responsible decision-making as *"the ability to make constructive and respectful choices about personal behavior and social interactions based on consideration of ethical standards, safety concerns, social norms, the realistic evaluation of consequences of various actions, and the well-being of self and others."* [144] Taken together, there is a wide range of evidence that providing opportunities for children and youth to make increasingly meaningful choices is critical to the development of self-regulation, values, and agency.[145]

Contributing. Ultimately, developmental experiences enable young people to contribute—to solve problems or bring into the world works of value to the self and others. Contributing is not only important because of its altruistic aspects and its value to a community. Contributing is also important developmentally. When young people have the opportunity to make meaningful contributions that are valued by others, they gain self-confidence and come to see themselves as capable.[146] Contributing to others gives our lives meaning. In a study of meaningfulness and happiness, researchers found that *"meaningfulness is associated with doing things for others,"* and that people who rated themselves as *"givers"* rather than *"takers"* had more meaningful lives.[147] Further, creating and contributing give young people the opportunity to practice agency. Contributing requires one to act with purpose, or to borrow John Dewey's words, to translate an *"original impulse and desire…into a plan and method of action"* to achieve one's desired end, based on *"observation, information, and judgment."* [148]

43

140 Abigail Baird, email communication with the authors, February 2015.
141 Deci & Ryan (1985); Ryan & Deci (2000).
142 Ryan & Deci (2006).
143 Erikson (1950/1963).
144 CASEL website (2015): http://www.casel.org/social-and-emotional-learning/core-competencies/.

145 Deci & Ryan (1985); Ryan & Deci (2000); National Research Council and Institute of Medicine (2004); Stefanou, Perencevich, DiCintio, & Turner (2004).
146 Hattie & Yates (2014).
147 Baumeister, Vohs, Aaker, & Garbinsky (2013, p. 512).
148 Dewey (1938, 1963, p. 69).

Contributing also makes clear that young people are not merely passive recipients of experience, nor are they powerless in the face of external forces that affect their lives. Schools and youth programs across the country are providing opportunities for young people to make genuine contributions that change material conditions in the world, for themselves and others. For example, youth leaders on Mikva Challenge's Juvenile Justice Council in Chicago saw the devastating effects that past arrest records had on young people's opportunities, particularly in communities of color. They learned that fewer than one-tenth of 1 percent of juvenile offenders got their records expunged when they became adults.[149] The Mikva youth leaders created an app—Expunge.io— that links youth who have juvenile records to pro bono lawyers who help them through the legal process to get their records erased at age 18. In another example, sixth-graders at Genesee Community Charter School in Rochester, New York, engaged in a year of research about the economic impacts that revitalized waterways had in four U.S. cities. They then successfully lobbied for a bond measure to restore the dry Erie Canal waterway that runs through downtown Rochester, based on their policy argument that the revitalized waterway would support restoration of a vibrant commercial district.[150] In yet another example, youth from Kids First! Oakland organized a multi-year campaign to win free or reduced-fare transit vouchers for low-income students so they could get to and from school.[151] The contributions of young people not only improve the lives of others, but also build critical competencies and develop agency for the young people themselves. Providing opportunities for these experiences is essential for youth development and learning.

The Reflective Aspect of Developmental Experiences: Making Meaning

John Dewey said, *"We do not learn from experience. We learn from reflecting on experience."*[152] As they move through their daily lives, children and youth engage in an ongoing process of interpretation and meaning-making, learning from a complex array of ideas, experiences, and interactions with others, and incorporating new information into their existing understanding of the world. It is through experience that youth develop the foundational components for success and a set of competencies. But if experience is to have lasting benefit, it must be assigned meaning and be integrated into one's emerging sense of identity. Psychologists as far back as William James in 1890 have noted that we can enhance learning by focusing our attention and reflecting on our experience. Research has consistently shown that learning is accelerated and more readily transferred to other situations when people reflect on what happened, what worked, and what needs improving.[153]

Critical to this process are strong, supportive, and sustained relationships with caring adults who can encourage young people to reflect on their experiences and help them to interpret those experiences in ways that expand their sense of themselves and their horizons. In this way, making sense of experience is an *"unrelentingly social"* process.[154] Mediating young people's thinking about their experience is one of the important ways that adults aid in learning and development.[155] Researchers have found that even young children are able to engage in metacognitive reflection and strategic thinking,[156] and benefit from adults and others who can help them reflect on their experience. In our conception of developmental experiences, we identify five particular types of reflection and meaning-making that support youth development: *describing, evaluating, connecting, envisioning,* and *integrating.*

Describing and Evaluating. Providing opportunities for young people to talk about and assess their lives, feelings, thoughts, and experiences is crucial to their overall development. Talking about an event or activity helps children to *"own"* the experience and define

---

149 Mikva Challenge (2014).
150 Expeditionary Learning (2014).
151 Kids First Oakland (2008).
152 Dewey (1938, p. 78).
153 Palincsar & Brown (1984); Scardamalia, Bereiter, & Steinbach (1984); Schoenfeld (1983, 1985, 1991).
154 Weick (1995, p. 79).
155 Bransford, Brown, & Cocking (2000); Vygotsky (1978).
156 Branford, Brown, & Cocking (2000); Brown & DeLoache (1978); DeLoache et al. (1998).

it for themselves. By putting words to experience, they can examine, categorize, evaluate, and decide what the experience means to them.

From the moment babies are born, adults facilitate language development by putting words to children's experience. We put names to things in the outside world (puppy, dump truck, pine tree) and to internal sensations and emotions (hungry, frustrated, silly). Adults' ongoing narration of the world has clear neurological and educational consequences for children. Differences in the variety and complexity of early caregivers' speech predict young children's future language development,[157] which in turn predicts self-regulatory ability and later academic achievement.[158] The richer the language children have to describe their experience, the more control they are able to exercise over themselves and the better able they are to articulate their needs and aspirations. Ultimately, *"we all make sense of the world with the discourses we have access to,"*[159] and this starts with infants' very first exposure to language.

As children get older, they play a more active role in narrating their experience. A practitioner in the Afterschool All-Stars program, William "BJ" Lohr, made this point when talking about the kids he works with. Beyond creating a physically and emotionally safe environment that invites children to participate, the next step is *"finding ways for [youth] to share their voice and engage and interact with the program in a meaningful way."*[160] Talking about the world is also how children build knowledge—and the more knowledge they build, the more able they are to participate in discussions about how things work. Describing the world and developing knowledge and awareness are reciprocal activities in a virtuous cycle.

Describing and evaluating one's experience also has important implications for developing mindsets. Social and developmental psychologists have studied the role of *"self-talk"* and attributions in shaping young people's attitudes about learning. If children conclude from

their early experiences that life is erratic and outside of their control, they can develop a mindset of *"learned helplessness"*[161] and refrain from exerting effort to improve their situation. If children conclude from their experiences that they are not smart enough to do well in school (what Carol Dweck and colleagues have called a *"fixed mindset"*), they will seek to avoid risk and withdraw effort, thus creating a self-fulfilling prophecy of poor performance.[162] Helping children and adolescents to reframe such experiences is critical for their long-term achievement in school, as mindsets tend to become self-reinforcing,[163] thus shaping young people's interpretations of their subsequent experiences.

Older youth have a particular need to talk about their ideas and feelings as they encounter more diverse points of view and develop abilities for more complex thought. Adolescents can begin to decipher better and worse options and to evaluate their own behaviors or performance. Dialogue not only fosters close social relationships and helps youth figure out their values and perspectives, it also creates the conditions for making change and exercising agency. This is at the heart of Paulo Freire's pedagogical philosophy. He pushed against the idea of simply narrating the world for young people (as happens in the traditional model of education), insisting instead that people *"achieve significance as human beings"* by *"naming the world [for themselves]…. Dialogue is thus an existential necessity."*[164]

Connecting. One of the key insights to emerge from the last few decades of research in cognitive science is that the human brain thinks in terms of *relationships*. To really understand something, young people have to see how it connects to other things they know. By *"relating a new item to an already known piece of knowledge, or otherwise…making an association with it,"* children make a *"major advance"* in their ability to commit information to memory.[165] This has important implications for developing knowledge—one of the foundational com-

45

157 Huttenlocher, Waterfall, Vasilyeva, Vevea, & Hedges (2010).
158 Petersen, Bates, & Staples (2015).
159 Smyth & Hattam (2001, p. 411).
160 UChicago CCSR interview with William "BJ" Lohr, consultant, After-School All Stars program (October 15, 2014).
161 Seligman (1972).
162 Dweck & Leggett (1988).
163 Yeager & Walton (2011).
164 Freire (1970/1993, p. 88).
165 Hattie & Yates (2014, p. 161).

ponents in the present framework. As children learn to group similar things together and organize information in larger conceptual frameworks, they also increase their ability to retrieve facts when needed. In a comprehensive review of *How People Learn,* John Bransford and his colleagues noted that a key distinction between experts and novices is that experts see patterns and relationships among the ideas in a field that the novice cannot see.[166] Understanding how things are connected allows experts to amass a huge volume of knowledge and quickly retrieve relevant information. Not only do novices know fewer facts, but they have more difficulty locating them when needed. Providing children with opportunities to connect new experiences and new ideas to things they already know is critical for building usable knowledge.

Creating connections not only helps to build cognitive understanding, but it also allows youth to direct their attention. As children grow, their developing brains utilize a complex network of synaptic connections linking cognition, emotion, and behavior. Perhaps out of self-preservation in a world that bombards us with continual stimuli, the brain only pays attention to things we see as interesting, relevant, or important. Researchers have found that the value individuals perceive in a given activity is directly related to their motivation to engage in and their ability to focus on that activity. For instance, the degree to which students perceive an academic task as having value is strongly linked to their choice, persistence, and performance of the task.[167] In an experiment in ninth-grade science classes, students completed monthly writing assignments about the science topics they were studying. One group was asked to write about how the science topic related to something they valued, and the control group was asked to write a summary of the science topic. At the end of the year, researchers compared the grades of the two groups. Among students who had low expectations for success at the beginning of the year, those in the group that connected science

to something they valued earned almost a full letter grade higher (0.8 grade points) than low-expectation students who wrote summaries.[168] The importance of connecting work to things people care about holds true in the workplace as well. A number of studies find that individuals are not only more motivated, but also more disciplined when their work is connected to pursuing personally meaningful goals.[169]

The opportunities that young people have to discover and develop a sense of the connection between their own interests and a larger social purpose reinforce related processes of motivation and self-regulation. Individuals who see tasks or activities as being connected to a larger social purpose are likely to engage with increased discipline, diligence, and persistence in pursuit of their objectives. Young people who are motivated and engaged in this way are more likely to succeed at the tasks and activities they undertake, perhaps underscoring a sense of self-efficacy as well as reinforcing the underlying value of what is accomplished. The recursive links between interest, purpose, value, motivation, self-regulation, and accomplishment are a potential basis for developing a durable, integrated identity over time. In the absence of connection to something they value, young people's commitments become brittle and difficult to sustain, particularly in the face of challenges, setbacks, or failures.

Envisioning. One of the most critical reflective experiences for young people is the act of envisioning themselves in the future. The precursor to this process can be seen in very young children engaged in imaginative play as they don a firefighter's hat, push a miniature grocery cart, care for dolls, or build with wooden hammers. Though young children may talk of being an astronaut or a veterinarian when they grow up, they have yet to develop the capacity for abstract thought that underlies the notion of *"becoming"* an adult. Toddlers are aware of daily routines, and by the age of four or five, typically developing children will

---

166 Bransford, Brown, & Cocking (2000).
167 Atkinson (1957); Damon (2008); Eccles et al. (1983); McKnight & Kashdan (2009); Wigfield (1994); Wigfield & Eccles (1992).
168 Hulleman & Harackiewicz (2009).
169 Yeager et al. (2014); see also, Fishbach & Trope (2005); Fishbach, Zhang, & Trope (2010); Mischel, Cantor, & Feldman (1996); Rachlin, Brown, & Cross (2000); Thaler & Shefrin (1981); Trope & Fishbach, (2000); Eccles (2009).

understand that time is a continuum, that some events have happened in the past and others will happen in the future.[170] But it is later in childhood and into early adolescence that a young person develops the ability to reflect on his or her thoughts, feelings, goals, and experiences in the past, present, and future—and recognize that there is the same and yet changing *"self"* across time. This awareness of the continuity of the self is key to understanding that actions at one point in time have consequences at another point in time.

Creating developmental opportunities for youth to envision their futures requires adults to understand the psychological processes underlying identity development. Human beings have a need for a sense of consistency and predictability that leads us to experience the self as relatively stable, but in fact psychological research shows self-concept to be changeable and sensitive to external cues.[171] In essence, we have many *"selves"* that develop in different contexts, with different social groups. Each of a young person's important social groups may have its own explanatory paradigm for making sense of the world and assigning one's place within it. Social groups act powerfully on young people's ability to envision their future and their sense of *"how high to aim."*[172] Berger and Luckmann refer to social groups as *"subuniverses of meaning"* because of their power to cue particular frames of reference, ideas of normative behavior, and an understanding of who one is and who one might become.[173] Psychologically speaking, particularly in early and middle adolescence, *"we can become the kind of person that people of our group can become [and] we fear disappointing important groups by failing to attain group norms and standards."*[174]

Research on "possible selves" suggests that, by itself, envisioning a positive future image of oneself is not enough to motivate behavior. Psychology professor Daphna Oyserman and her colleagues argue that particular conditions must be in place in order for envisioning to lead to improved outcomes for youth.

First, young people not only need positive images of what they want to become, but also negative visions of what they want to avoid becoming.[175] Second, these positive and negative *"future possible selves"* must be linked to specific behaviors or strategies that will either bring about or prevent the realization of such selves in the future.[176] Young people are most likely to regulate their current behavior when they know what is likely to move them toward their positive future vision and what kinds of behaviors are likely to derail them. In order for adolescents to embark on positive paths toward their envisioned future, possible selves and the behaviors that lead to them need to be reconciled with young people's important social identities.[177] Social inequalities and stereotypes can create significant hurdles for low-income minority youth, making it difficult to picture themselves as academically successful or to engage in behaviors that would bring about such success.[178] Adults can play a critical developmental role by helping young people to envision a concrete, positive future that *embraces* their important social identities.

Two additional notes are important in helping young people to envision and pursue positive futures. First, the multiple social identities that youth maintain (e.g., daughter, point guard on the girls' basketball team, future pediatrician, younger sister, good science student, retail sales clerk at the mall, friend in a group of outspoken girls) and the associated norms of thought and behavior associated with each identity make it impossible to keep all of this autobiographical information *"on line"* simultaneously. Oyserman explains that what is present in one's working memory at any given point is likely to be what is *"cued"* or called forth by the present context.[179] The self-concept a girl experiences on the basketball court may be very different from her self-concept when encountering her big brother's friends in the neighborhood. Second, across contexts, humans seek to maintain a sense of positive regard for the self.[180] This means that youth will interpret situations in a way that allows them to feel

47

170 Curtis (1998).
171 Markus & Kunda (1986); Swann (1997).
172 Harvey & Schroder (1963).
173 Berger & Luckmann (1966); Oyserman & Markus (1998).
174 Oyserman & Fryberg (2006, p. 21).
175 Oyserman & Markus (1990).

176 Oyserman, Terry, & Bybee (2002).
177 Oyserman & James (2011).
178 Espinoza-Herold (2003); Labov (1982); Oyserman (2008); Oyserman, Bybee, & Terry (2006).
179 Oyserman (2001).
180 Rogers (1959); Weick (1995).

competent and keep their self-esteem intact. When they find themselves in a context in which they are performing poorly (e.g., in a school setting in which they are not being academically successful), children and youth are likely to *"subvert"* that setting in some way to restore a positive sense of themselves, creating *"counter-definitions of reality and identity."* [181] For example, a poorly performing student may discount the importance of academic success or of the particular task at hand (*"This is a stupid assignment anyway!"*) to protect his self-concept. Alternatively, he may reframe the classroom not as an academic setting in which he performs poorly, but as a social setting in which he is popular and has desirable status.

If an envisioning activity is conducted in a context that does not cue the kinds of self-conceptions that would lead to positive behaviors—for example, in a high school classroom where teenagers have imposed their own social reality—then the envisioning activity is likely to be unsuccessful. For envisioning to be a productive developmental experience, adults need to pay attention to creating a supportive context that will embrace young people's important social identities and integrate those identities with positive future visions.

Integrating. Ultimately the goal of any developmental experience is to integrate the insights, developing skills, or other lessons the experience generates into one's larger sense of self in a way that expands a young person's competencies and agency in the world. This is particularly important throughout adolescence, as young people engage with the task of constructing a cohesive identity. While younger children can make connections to feelings, experiences, or potential roles, adolescents can integrate these into a sense of themselves. For example, as teenagers experience success in one arena, particularly after some amount of struggle, integration means applying that success to inform a larger sense of who they are and what they are capable of. Integration moves a young person from a stance of *"I did that"* to embrace a larger implication for one's identity: *"I'm the kind of person who*

can…" Again, adults play an important role in helping young people incorporate their experiences and accomplishments into a cohesive vision of themselves.

Integration of one's social identities can have specific performance advantages. When different social identities are not integrated, a person might not have access to bodies of knowledge or modes of behavior that she possesses, if such knowledge and behavior are associated with a social identity that is not being cued in the present situation. For example, researchers found that the performance of Asian women on academic tests depended on whether their gender identity or their cultural identity was cued at the time of the test. Activating their gender identity resulted in lower math scores and higher verbal scores, while activating their Asian identity resulted in higher math scores and lower verbal scores. [182] This line of research suggests that *"even though one might theoretically possess the expertise or know-how to solve a problem, certain knowledge systems may not be accessible at a given time because the relevant social identity is not activated."* [183] Some researchers theorize that individuals with higher levels of identity integration should be better at activating multiple social identities simultaneously, which should then give them simultaneous access to the different knowledge systems associated with each social identity. [184] Following this line of thought, young people who are able to integrate various experiences and the lessons learned from those experiences into an integrated sense of self should be better able to draw on the full range of their experience to inform their actions in a wide range of settings.

The box entitled *Youth Profile: Ana* illustrates what the process of developmental experiences, including the processes of meaning-making, can look like for a high-school aged youth. In a youth theater group, Ana encountered new ways of being in the world, was able to connect her own life experience with larger social issues, had opportunities to tinker and practice as part of preparing a theater production, and came to envision new possibilities for herself.

---

181   Berger & Luckmann (1966, p. 153).
182   Shih, Pittinsky, & Ambady (1999).
183   Cheng, Sanchez-Burks, & Lee (2008, pp. 1178-1179).
184   Cheng, Sanchez-Burks, & Lee (2008).

48

Ana

At age 13, Ana was a studious and sensitive girl, talkative around people she knew well, but not a natural performer. But the summer before her eighth-grade year, encouraged by a friend, she walked to a nearby park field house and signed up for a series of free workshops led by Chicago Youth Theater.

Right from the start, she encountered new ways of interacting with other people. At first, the physical contact required by many of the theater exercises intimidated Ana. She recalls one that required pairs to sit back-to-back on the floor with their arms hooked and try to stand up. But she observed how uninhibited the older students who were long-time ensemble members seemed. *"Everyone seemed OK with holding hands or locking arms and stuff,"* she says. *"Everyone seemed comfortable with each other."*

In school, she was shy. She says, *"I just wasn't good at working with people. I just kind of kept to myself a lot."*

But the theater workshops gave her a chance to experiment with new ways of expressing herself through her body and voice and to collaborate with peers in improvising a scene.

As she observed and experimented, the daring of the ensemble members began to rub off on her. She says, *"It was a lot of putting yourself out there, being yourself, and being really goofy. In school people hold themselves back a lot, and people here just let themselves go. It was weird but comforting at the same time."*

The company creates original productions based on true stories gathered from cast members, their families, and neighbors in the multi-ethnic community. She joined when she was a freshman in high school, and the theme for that year's production was immigration.

As a first step, the company members sat in a circle and shared their own knowledge of the topic.

Ana's parents are Mexican immigrants and her father is in danger of deportation, which is a constant source of stress in her own life. But as the company shared their stories, interviewed neighbors, and then traveled around the city to hear other stories from immigration activists, Ana realized that she was not alone. She was able to reflect on her experience and connect her family's situation to larger social and public policy issues. With the directors, she and other students attended rallies as participants, like one to stop a deportation center from being built.

During the rallies and the interviews, she listened to adults who were immigrants or activists describe and evaluate their own experiences with immigration.

She integrated what she learned into her own belief system. *"You slowly find out what you believe in and what you don't,"* she says. *"Immigration is an issue I'm always going to be passionate about. If it wasn't for Chicago Youth Theater, I wouldn't know how strongly I feel about it."*

As the interviews progressed, the directors selected the most compelling material from the transcripts for the company to read through and discuss. Next came improvisation assignments based on the transcripts. Company members tinkered for months with staging, characters, movement, and sound. The improvisations were video recorded and later incorporated by the directors into a final script.

49

Mounting a full-scale production required a tremendous amount of practice with feedback from the directors, continuing even after opening night. This was especially true for Ana as her tenure in the company grew and she took on more demanding roles.

At the end of her junior year, she played a woman who, with her husband, rescues a niece from an abusive home. The role was a pivotal one, as the aunt and uncle's love is what transforms the young girl's life.

"I've never been one who exposes my feelings," Ana explains. *"It was hard. I just had to strip away that shell and be open."*

A sense of a higher purpose motivated her to persevere, despite her frustration with the challenging emotional content, until she finally broke through. *"It was for the story,"* she says, *"not how comfortable I felt hugging people or looking in people's eyes showing emotions. It was for the audience members to really get this."* Ana's desire to contribute to the audience's understanding allowed her to transcend her own discomfort.

Beginning her sophomore year, the directors began to encourage Ana to think about college. Although a strong student, Ana, whose parents left school at a young age, had never considered it. But her encounters with college through college tours with the company, college counseling with the directors, and talking with ensemble members who were becoming first generation college students, she began to envision a different future for herself. *"When you're in a group of friends and they get all excited for college and they're ready for it, it influences you,"* says Ana, who applied to college this fall. *"It assured me I'm capable of doing it."*

50

Summary of Developmental Experiences

In summary, developmental experiences that provide young people with opportunities to act and reflect constitute the raw material from which the foundational components and key factors of young adult success are built. Developmental experiences are those that expose young people to new ideas, people, and perspectives; provide opportunities to engage in hands-on learning; include demonstrations of expert performance and models of high quality work to emulate; offer extended time to practice and develop competencies; and ultimately allow young people to contribute their unique gifts to the world. Further, developmental experiences offer opportunities to reflect upon one's learning, to *"name the world,"* to evaluate ideas, and to make connections between one's actions and other things one cares about. Finally, developmental experiences support young people in integrating disparate occurrences into a larger sense of themselves in a way that propels them forward.

Developmental experiences thus set the stage for acting with agency in the world in an ongoing cycle.

Importantly, although each type of experience has been presented one-by-one in this chapter, in reality, youth often engage in numerous types of experiences simultaneously and there is no hierarchy of complexity or suggested ordering for the types of experiences. **The box entitled** *Developmental Experiences Align with the Connected Learning Approach* **illustrates an alignment between the framework of Connected Learning and the concept of developmental experiences.**[185] Indeed, *"when a concrete experience is enriched by reflection, given meaning by thinking, and transformed by action, the new experience created becomes richer, broader, and deeper."*[186] Developmental experiences often occur in the context of youth's interactions with adults and other children, and these social relationships are the instruments through which adults can guide and shape development.

51

Developmental Experiences Align with the Connected Learning Approach

This chapter discusses a range of action and reflection opportunities that help youth feel connected to their experiences and make meaning of them. Although each of these opportunities has been presented as distinct (e.g., opportunities to encounter, and then to tinker, and then to practice, and then to choose), in practice, high-quality experiences for youth entail combinations of actions and reflections every day. Youth programs and school-based interactions should be built around providing multiple, ongoing opportunities for such experiences.

One approach that supports this idea is called *"connected learning."*[187] Connected learning brings together adolescents' learning experiences across in-school and out-of-school spaces, purporting that youth learn best when learning is *"socially embedded, interest-driven, and oriented towards education, economic, or political opportunity."*[188] Ito and her colleagues argue that youth are engaged in their own learning only when it is driven by their interests. Such experiences and learning can then be connected to educational or career opportunities or civic engagement.

The connected learning approach suggests that youth need spaces to make contributions and share their work with peers; to be driven in their work by their individual interests and build expertise in areas they value as significant to themselves; and to have people around them who can make the necessary connections between their interests and academic domains/institutions. Connected learning *"seeks to integrate three spheres of learning that are often disconnected and at war with each other in young people's lives: peer culture, interests, and academic content".*[189] These experiences can help make youth's experiences hold more meaning and relevance for them, and connect these interests and experiences with future-orientated images of themselves.

The design principles identified in a recent report on Connected Learning align closely with the notion of developmental experiences for youth. They highlight the need for active participation by youth; learning by being given the opportunity to *do* (or practice); having adults who provide appropriate challenges to push youth in areas in which they have deep interest; and support in making connections between what youth are experiencing within their interest-driven activities and other external academic and cultural experiences.

---

185 Ito, Gutiérrez, Livingstone, Penuel, Rhodes, & Salen (2013).
186 Kolb & Kolb (2009, p. 309).
187 Ito et al. (2013).

188 Ito et al. (2013, p. 42).
189 Ito et al. (2013, p. 63).

Developmental Relationships as Critical Contexts for Learning

Cutting across the literature on child and youth development is a consistent emphasis on the importance of social relationships. Social interactions provide children with opportunities to enact behaviors, elicit feedback, and reflect on what happens. To the degree that activity and reflection are consistently guided in strong, supportive, and sustained relationships with adults, they provide critical opportunities for children to experiment, learn, and grow within and across the various contexts they inhabit every day. Where those opportunities are lacking—where children have few chances to interact or experience the world, where feedback is poor, where reflection is hampered in one fashion or another—children's ability to integrate novel experiences and increasingly complex learning into their identities is often blocked. The iterative and fundamentally relational processes of experiencing, interacting, and reflecting represent a critical engine for children's development and as such are the core of the conceptual model linking experiences and relationships with young adult success.

Developmental experiences offer multiple opportunities for adults to play important supportive roles in building youth's self-regulation, knowledge and skills, mindsets, and values. Social relationships are important not only in supplying broader access to opportunity, but also as a means through which young people learn about themselves and their place in the wider world. One well-adopted theory, called situated learning theory, argues that learning does not happen in an abstract sense; rather, it always emerges as part of a transaction between a young person and his or her social environment.[190] In this way, knowledge does not so much reside *"in the head"* of an individual, but rather within a *"community of practice"* into which young people can be apprenticed. This notion of apprenticeship provides a helpful metaphor for thinking about developmental relationships.

The developmental role of social relationships starts from the earliest moments of life. Interactions between infants and early caregivers form the basis for infants' emotional experiences and set the stage for future relationships. The level of attachment security set in infancy (secure versus insecure attachments) remains largely stable through adolescence.[191] A stable and responsive caregiver strengthens an infant's developing agency and self-efficacy by allowing for exploration in a stable and safe environment.[192] Learning how to manage brief and moderate stress, such as hunger or discomfort, is a part of healthy development, and attachment to stable and responsive adults ameliorates the distress a young child experiences with such stressors.[193] As children mature, relationships grow in sophistication and variety, becoming both more important and more complex. The centrality of family relationships gives way somewhat as children enter school and spend increasing amounts of time with peers. Non-familial adults also become increasingly important. The character and quality of relationships can vary substantially across the life course as young people's inclination and capacity to engage socially with others deepen and become more central to their growing sense of self.

Drawing from Bronfenbrenner's[194] description of optimal relationships, Li and Julian define four criteria for *developmental relationships*—attachment, reciprocity, progressive complexity, and balance of power—that they argue *"consistently promote positive development*

---

190 Lave & Wenger (1991); Vygotsky (1978).

191 Center on the Developing Child (2004); Hamilton (2000); National Research Council and Institute for Medicine (2000); Thompson (2008).

192 National Research Council and Institute for Medicine (2000).

193 In the absence of secure attachments with stable and responsive adults, strong, frequent, or prolonged exposure to stress in the early years can have damaging effects on learning, behavior, and health for years to come (Center on the Developing Child, 2012; Fox, Almas, Degnan, Nelson, & Zeanah, 2011; Shonkoff, 2011). Neural circuits for responding to stress and threats are particularly susceptible to early experiences (Davis et al., 2007; Huizink, Robles de Medina, Mulder, Visser, & Buitelaar, 2003; Weinstock, 2005). Prenatal experiences and early exposure to stress can result in a person being overly reactive or completely shutting down in reaction to stressful situations throughout the lifespan (Loman & Gunnar, 2010; Shonkoff, 2011). These long-term consequences also have important implications for executive functioning and working memory in older children and adolescents (Shonkoff, 2011; Evans & Schamberg, 2009).

194 Bronfenbrenner (1979).

52

for children and youth across diverse developmental settings." [195] Building upon this work, researchers at the Search Institute have laid out a framework describing developmental relationships as a locus not only for communicating and providing care and support to youth as they grow, but also as a critical site for expressing challenge and expanding opportunities. [196]

The Search Institute framework highlights five elements of developmental relationships to serve as guideposts for adults in schools and other youth-serving organizations—and that dovetail with the key components of developmental experiences outlined above. First, developmental relationships create opportunities for adults to **express care**—to be present, warm, invested, interested, and dependable. Second, developmental relationships are a key site in which to **challenge growth**—to inspire, to express clear expectations, to stretch thinking, and to set and enforce appropriate boundaries and limits. Third, developmental relationships provide a space in which to communicate and **provide support**—to encourage, to guide, to model, and to advocate on youths' behalf. Fourth, developmental relationships represent an important venue in which to **share power**—to demonstrate respect, to give voice and listen carefully, to respond thoughtfully, and to collaborate openly with youth. Finally, developmental relationships provide a key avenue through which to **expand possibilitie**s—to explore new ideas and experiences, to connect youth to helpful others, and to navigate challenging experiences or barriers that deflect youth from their goals.

Blair Root, the director of a youth neighborhood club, emphasized the importance of children having developmental relationships with multiple adults that provide opportunities to act and reflect. *"I think it's important that kids have different role models in their lives for different reasons. Maybe they think their art teacher is so cool because she introduced them to so many neat things, and their dad at home, maybe he's a cool engineer and they're able to share different experiences together."*

Connected to this view of developmental relationships is a vision of those relationships as being reciprocal. In being so, youth not only passively receive or access the various kinds of resources and opportunities created by virtue of their social relationships, but also have opportunities to participate actively in the larger contexts within which those relationships occur and to contribute positively to them. UChicago CCSR's review of noncognitive factors in school performance noted that the belief that one is recognized and valued as a member of an academic community is key to engaging and succeeding in that context. [197] This sense of *"belonging"* has been associated with success in school, [198] while feeling unwelcome or threatened has been associated with poorer performance, as seen in the literature on stereotype threat [199] and bullying. [200]

Research by Scales, Benson, and Roehlkepartain addresses how the reciprocal path of developmental relationships relates to the concept of thriving. [201] Thriving, particularly during adolescence, focuses attention on young people's self-identified *"sparks"*— passions, interests, skills—and creates opportunities to support, develop, and nurture them over time. [202] The nurturing of one's passions is key to the development of a *"confident and secure idealized personhood,"* [203] similar in many respects to our concept of integrated identity. The focus on thriving illustrates the reciprocal nature of developmental relationships, with an emphasis on nurture and support, on the one hand, and on the creation of opportunities for participation and contribution, on the other. Reciprocal relation-

---

195 Li & Julian (2012, p. 157).
196 Search Institute (2014).
197 Farrington et al. (2012).
198 Osterman (2000).
199 Steele (1997); Steele & Aronson (1995).
200 Elias & Zins (2012).
201 Scales, Benson, & Roehlkepartain (2011).

202 See also Benson (2008); Benson & Scales (2009). The notion of attending to youth's own interests is also in line with the Connected Learning theory (Ito et al., 2013); see box *Developmental Experiences Align with the Connected Learning Approach* on page 51.
203 Scales, Benson, & Roehlkepartain (2010, p. 264); Lerner, Brentano, Dowling, & Anderson (2002).

ships may be especially critical during developmental transitions, such as the transition from middle grades into high school, when the task of negotiating the shifting boundaries between connection and autonomy can leave youth more vulnerable.[204]

Social relationships provide important opportunities for youth to sharpen their awareness of themselves, others, and the larger environment. Strong, supported, and sustained relationships with caring adults provide an important space for youth to experiment, try out roles and behaviors, and receive feedback that helps to shape how they ultimately construct an integrated identity. As youth work toward an understanding and articulation of their goals and values, the feedback and opportunities for reflection provided by social relationships with adults provide a key avenue for the development and integration of identity, as well as the formation and support of mindsets, the development of competencies, and the building of agency. Creating a social context that supports the development of the foundational components and key factors for young adult success requires not only careful and intentional planning by adults, but also long-term commitment to young people in their care.

Enactment of Developmental Practices

The cumulative theory and evidence on developmental experiences and developmental relationships means that educators, mentors, and program staff would do well to extend their attention beyond design and planning, and to focus on understanding youth experience. Within any given setting that children and youth inhabit, adults generally have positive intentions and want to act in the best interests of the young people with whom they work. In formal settings such as schools and youth-serving organizations, adult practices are largely planned in order to effect positive change in kids' lives. Despite these intentions, a key consideration is how practices actually get delivered by the teachers, program staff, parents, or other caregivers—in other

words, the *enactment* of the plans and intentions via the practices of adults in the setting. What actually occurs in the moments when adults and youth interact may or may not align with either best intentions or the description of practices as set forth by planners.

Any time an adult puts a practice in place, it is influenced by a plethora of adult-, youth-, and situation-specific characteristics. How an adult actually enacts a practice can be shaped by the adult's personal orientations, how well the adult is able to interact with particular youth, and even the adult's *own* development of the foundational components we highlight for youth (e.g., self-regulation, knowledge and skills, mindsets, or values). Enactment can also be shaped by the training, experience, assumptions, capacities, and *"working theories"* that adults in a setting bring individually to their work. For example, some teachers might believe that young people in urban environments will benefit most from a *"tough love"* approach that prepares them for the harsh realities of the outside world, so they are particularly strict in enforcing policies around attendance or late work. Other teachers in the same school might believe that these same young people most need nurturance and warm relationships with trusted adults, so they enforce school-wide tardy and late work policies much more leniently. Some parents might believe that young children benefit most from unstructured play and opportunities to be creative, while other parents believe it is critical to take a strict, disciplined approach to academics as soon as possible with young children. Sometimes conflicting beliefs are held by caregivers within the same organization or the same family, and these individual biases or preferences come through regardless of the pedagogical or childrearing approach the caregivers might have mutually agreed to.

The *"official"* orientations and practices endorsed by a school, a youth program, or even a family may have less influence on a child's development than the ways practices are actually enacted "in the moment" by the adults in those settings and experienced by the child. A daycare program may endorse the practice of modeling positive

---

204 Scales, Benson, & Roehlkepartain (2011, p. 265); Collins & Steinberg (2006).

54

problem-solving for young children, but the daycare provider may (unintentionally) raise her voice and become harsh when she feels stressed. A harried father might put great value on punctuality, but in practice he might often be late to pick up his child from school. It is therefore critical that adults pay close attention to how intended practices are actually enacted within a given setting. Ultimately, it is not the intention but the enactment that influences the experiences young people have and the meaning they make of those experiences.

Differences in Developmental Opportunities and Needs

Daily life provides no end of experiences that help children exercise self-regulation, develop knowledge and skills, shape their mindsets, and build their values. But we know that *"daily life"* can vary substantially for young people across race and class. Children in the United States are afforded different access to experiences and opportunities in their homes, schools, and communities, depending in large part on differences in financial resources. An extensive body of prior research documents the negative effects of child poverty, which extend well beyond low socioeconomic status and include a wide array of associated conditions, including heightened social isolation, greater levels of parental and child stress, limited parental investment (of both money and time) in children's development, less access to health care, higher exposure to environmental toxins, and lower academic achievement.[205] As of 2012, one out of five children ages 5 to 17 in the United States was living in poverty. Roughly one-third of all African American, Latino, and Native American children grow up in poor households.[206] While families in poverty are often rich in other developmental assets (e.g., strong familial ties, dual languages, strong narrative traditions, entrepreneurial skills, and other valuable *"funds of knowledge"*[207]), we know that differences by income in parental investment in children's informal education—for example, through sports clubs, summer camp, travel, and computers and books in the home—show

evidence of contributing to gaps in academic achievement that are observed upon entry to formal schooling and widen as students advance through school.[208]

Children who grow up in more affluent families do not necessarily have *"better"* developmental experiences, just more of them. It is important to emphasize that *"high culture"* activities that are more readily available to the children of upper-middle-class families may not be developmentally superior to activities more easily accessed by low-income urban or rural children. Looking for frogs in a drainage ditch can meet a child's need for exploration, discovery, and knowledge-building just as well as a trip to the science museum. Still, compounded differences in the availability of high-quality early childhood programs, effective and engaging K-12 schools, books in the home, after school activities, libraries, music and arts programs, sports and recreational activities, and museums and other cultural institutions end up significantly favoring children from wealthier families.[209] Ensuring that *all* young people have access to a multitude of rich developmental experiences—from early childhood through adolescence—is imperative to helping youth develop the key factors for success in young adulthood and the foundational components that underlie those factors.

A further advantage that accrues to the children of wealthier families has to do with their early acculturation into dominant cultural norms and settings. All children grow up learning cultural navigation skills that allow them to move with relative ease around their own neighborhoods and communities,[210] but those skills do not always readily transfer to new contexts. A white child from the wealthy Chicago suburb of Winnetka would be just as out of place and ill-equipped to make his way through the violence-plagued streets of Chicago's Roseland neighborhood as would the Roseland native in Winnetka. The difference is that the child from Winnetka can go his whole life without having to learn how to navigate Roseland, but the child from Roseland cannot gain access to *"cultures of power"* in American life[211] without figuring out how to navigate Winnetka.

205 Berliner (2009); Yoshikawa, Aber, & Beardslee (2012).
206 Aud et al. (2012).
207 González, Moll, & Amanti (2005).
208 Kaushal, Magnuson, & Waldfogel (2011).

209 Lareau (2003).
210 Lareau (2003); Patton (2013).
211 Delpit (1988, 1995).

55

Children who grow up learning dominant conventions and behavioral norms that are also in operation in schools and workplaces have more ready access to these institutions. In this way, low-income and minority youth have to learn additional skills—the ability to navigate other social contexts—and have to integrate more disparate identities to be on equal footing with children who were born into the dominant social culture.

In light of children and youth's differing needs and developmental opportunities, adults are challenged to figure out how best to support the development of each child and coordinate this development across settings. Critical to achieving this goal is providing teachers, parents, childcare workers, program providers, and other caregivers with both knowledge about *what matters* at each developmental stage and strategies for creating thoughtful and intentional developmental experiences. Though experiences are the fields within which children develop, they aren't enough to ensure that children are building the foundational components for future success. One of the objectives of this project is to help program developers, practitioners, and caregivers think more intentionally about how the practices they are implementing are, or can be, aligned with the developmental outcomes they are trying to support in children and youth, given their individual needs. It is in the context of strong and supportive social relationships with adults and peers that children learn to make meaning of their experience, come to understand themselves in relation to others, and situate themselves in the world.

56

CHAPTER 3

Developmental Progression Toward Young Adulthood

⊙ Key Points

///

- Development is multifaceted (social, emotional, attitudinal, behavioral, cognitive, physical), and each aspect of development is inextricably connected to the others.

- To provide the most appropriate and supportive developmental experiences for youth, adults need to understand development itself as well as how to match the right supports and sets of challenges for growth to the particular developmental stage of the youth they work with.

- The practices of adults are more effective when they are intentional, are focused on the foundational components and key factors that support the ability to transition successfully into young adulthood, and take a developmental perspective. The development of the key factors of young adult success (agency, integrated identity, and competencies) and the four foundational components that underlie them (self-regulation, knowledge and skills, mindsets, and values) occur at different rates for different individuals from early childhood through young adulthood.

- Consistent and supportive interactions with care-givers provide the greatest opportunity for cognitive stimulation in ways that can have long-lasting impacts on children's development. Whereas appropriate stimulation supports continuing development, a lack of stimulation can create barriers to subsequent development, potentially requiring more intensive intervention later.

- Key tasks of each developmental stage are listed be-low. However, it is crucial that adults not *exclude* other areas of development when engaging with children and youth; nearly every aspect of the foundational components and key factors is forming, or is at least being influenced by the experiences youth encounter, at every stage of life.

- In brief, the key developmental tasks during early-life stages of development are:
  - Early childhood (ages 3 to 5): Self-regulation; interpersonal (social-emotional) knowledge and skills
  - Middle childhood (ages 6 to 10): Self-regulation (self-awareness and self-control); learning-related skills and knowledge; interpersonal skills
  - Early adolescence (ages 11 to 14): Group-based identity; emerging mindsets
  - Middle adolescence (ages 15 to 18): Sense of values; individuated identity
  - Young adulthood (ages 19 to 22): Integrated identity

- A successful transition into young adulthood relies on a firm footing of the foundational components: an awareness of self and others to support self-regulation and planning; knowledge and skills about self and the world, developed at home and through school and other learning activities; mindsets that project a self-belief and support one's agency to achieve goals; the values a person holds for self and society; and the identity choices one makes, hopefully based on a broad sampling of possibilities.

///

The Foundations for Young Adult Success developmental framework includes four components (self-regulation, knowledge and skills, mindsets, and values) that provide the foundation for three key factors in young adulthood (agency, integrated identity, and competencies). The framework highlights the crucial role played by developmental experiences and developmental relationships within the larger contexts that young people inhabit. It is important to note that development is *always* occurring, whether with intentional support and carefully constructed opportunities for positive growth or not. Individual, contextual, and larger structural forces continually interact to shape the course of one's development across all stages of childhood and adolescence.[212]

Developmental relationships help stretch young

---

212 Bronfenbrenner (1979).

people to be the best versions of themselves. When interactions between caregivers and children are intentional and informed, as well as organized to provide experiential opportunities for growth, they are more likely to support positive learning and development and lead to a young adulthood with agency, an integrated identity, and a set of competencies that enable success. However, in order to design and deliver the most effective experiences for youth, it is imperative to understand where youth are *developmentally* throughout their young lives. This understanding makes it possible for adults to match experiences and interactions to the developmental needs of young people.

In considering what we know about how children develop, this chapter focuses on how each of the foundational components and key factors matures over time. As documented in the literature, different skills develop at different rates over the life course. Below, we highlight the most prevalent areas of growth during each stage of development, with an eye toward (1) which foundational components or key factors are most influenced by input, experiences, and interactions with others at each stage; and (2) which components or key factors need to be developed during the earlier stages to facilitate positive development at later stages. The chapter provides an overview of current knowledge based on a review of the literature and discussions with experts from a range of backgrounds.[213] This overview is not meant to be a comprehensive or exhaustive discussion of development. Rather, the goal is to provide practitioners with access to a common description of how the foundational components and key factors develop over time and which ones are the primary foci during each stage of development.[214]

We start our examination of development at the preschool years, at age three, when children begin to be exposed to institutions outside their families and homes. We then present the most salient and malleable areas of development during four life stages leading up to young adulthood: early childhood (ages 3 to 5), middle childhood (ages 6 to 10), early adolescence (ages 11 to 14), and middle adolescence (ages 15 to 18). For each stage, we ask four questions:

1. What internal or external changes are taking place that influence development in this stage?

2. What are the primary areas of development in this stage?

3. How do experiences shape development in this stage?

4. How is development in this stage related to development in other stages?

We conclude by discussing how development in these four stages culminates in preparing youth for a successful transition into young adulthood (between the ages of 19 to 22), highlighting how effective supports throughout the years increase the likelihood of a youth having agency, an integrated identity, and strong competencies. We pay particular attention to identity development and integration. This chapter specifically touches on how identity matures from one stage to the next, even if it is not a *key* developmental task during a particular stage. As a preview, the serious development of identity does not begin to take place until adolescence, but the antecedents are there from the earliest days of life:

A mature understanding of identity requires being able to connect and find patterns in one's actions and beliefs across time and situations, actively associating with these underlying traits, and viewing the self as purposefully creating such continuity in behavior. Given the complex nature of these cognitions, identity development disproportionately takes place during adolescence. However children begin to form concepts of the self and agency much earlier in life, and these serve as precursors to identity.[215]

---

213 A more extensive discussion of the key areas of development across stages of early life can be found in a memo drafted by UChicago CCSR, which can be obtained from the authors by request.

214 Admittedly, the quantity and quality of evidence around each of these life stages is uneven; one of the main tasks in reviewing the research evidence to date has been to identify areas in which broad understanding is yet incomplete.

215 Rote & Smetana (2014, p. 438).

Each of the following sections describes the primary developmental tasks as they relate to the foundational components and key factors, and explores the implications of those tasks for supporting youth development. Although we highlight key tasks in each developmental stage, it is crucial that adults not *exclude* other areas of development when engaging with children and youth; nearly every aspect of the foundational components is forming, or is at least being influenced, at every stage of life.

Early Childhood
(Preschool-Aged Children; Ages 3 to 5)

Early childhood—roughly ages 3 to 5—is a stage of tremendous growth and development. It is during this period that young children build upon their earliest interactions with parents and other caregivers and begin to feel a sense of independence, while learning how to identify and regulate their emotions and behaviors. According to Erikson's stages of psychosocial development, young children struggle with initiative vs. guilt.[216] In other words, children want to start setting their own goals and deciding their own actions. When adults around them give support and guidance, young children likely achieve a sense of purpose and some degree of agency, at least within the small sphere of their influence. However, when adults do not allow children to develop their own initiative, children may have a deep sense of guilt about their desires to act.

Key Questions
What Internal or External Changes Are Taking Place that Influence Development in Early Childhood?

The grounding for children's expansion of abilities lies within the brain as it changes and develops in response to children's experiences. The growth and molding of young children's brains are responsible for the more basic elements of coordination, movement, and alertness, as well as higher-order activities such as abstraction, inhibition, and planning.[217] Because of the neurological advances taking place during early childhood, including rapid development of the prefrontal cortex, preschool-aged children often experience newfound capabilities in writing, physical coordination, memory, regulation and inhibition, and even metacognition; they become able to explain why they took a series of actions, for example.[218] Though the prefrontal cortex does not fully develop until an individual's mid-20s, the foundation created in early childhood is critical for ongoing development.[219]

In addition to the development of cognition, young children are learning about emotions and how to interact with other people. Crucial to later identity development, preschool-aged children are developing a sense of self; they understand that they are different from others and are able to define themselves as such in increasingly concrete terms. In addition to an increasingly concrete sense of self, young children also develop gross and fine motor skills during this period. Often in parallel with an emerging sense of identity, children manifest an increasingly sophisticated sense of their own agency, which began in infancy. They know that they can invoke actions that will lead to something else happening, particularly around using objects. As we will see, the *"world"* in which a child exercises agency will continue to broaden as he or she gets older.

What Are the Primary Areas of Development in Early Childhood?

Researchers and practitioners who work with young children suggest that there are two key areas of development on which to focus support during the early childhood years: self-regulation and social-emotional skills—or the ability to interact well with other children (overlapping with our notion of interpersonal skills). (See Figure 5). Barbara Abel, a curriculum manager for Educare Chicago, an early education program, highlights how focusing on these areas is crucial, as young children can only begin to learn content once their social and emotional needs have been addressed:

59

---

216   Erikson (1950/1963).
217   Berk (2007).
218   Diamond (2000).
219   Diamond & Lee (2011).

For me, the main thing I've been working on is children's capacities to self-regulate. And when I say self-regulation I mean self-regulation in terms of emotional regulation, behavioral regulation, and attention regulation...I lead with the emphasis on the social-emotional in order to get to the point of being able to access the cognitive processes. —Barbara Abel, curriculum manager, Educare Chicago[220]

Self-Regulation. Early childhood represents an important opportunity to help children develop self-regulation, including behavioral, attentional, and emotional regulation.[221] Self-regulation enables a young child to begin acting independently within her personal and social context and to have greater success with learning.[222] Underlying the development of self-regulation is an improvement in executive function (EF) skills (see section in Chapter 1 entitled *Self-Regulation* for further description). The emergence and early development of EF skills correlate closely with the early development of the prefrontal cortex, described in the previous section; the brain continues to refine these new neural connections and EF skills into adolescence.[223]

Developing control over emotions, behaviors, and attention early in life is the basis for engaging in increasingly complex thinking and more multifaceted interactions as children develop. Among young children, self-regulation—particularly emotion regulation—is related to a more successful transition into schooling,[224] an early indicator for later academic success. Children who are able to monitor and manage their emotions and behaviors

FIGURE 5

Early Childhood (Preschool, Ages 3-5)

are better able to follow directions, cooperate with other children, and attend to what they are learning. Research also links early EF skills to later success in the workforce, in health, and in social relationships.[225] Conversely, the lack of early emotion and behavior regulation is linked to adult crime, violence, and other negative behaviors.[226]

Interpersonal Knowledge and Skills. The other key developmental task during early childhood is the development of knowledge and skills that support young children's abilities to relate to, cooperate with, and form relationships with other people, particularly other children. During the preschool years, children further develop their earlier understanding that there is a *"self"* and can distinguish their own from others' emotions. Children begin to understand that others can have

220 UChicago CCSR interview with Barbara Abel, curriculum manager, Educare, Chicago (April 21, 2014).
221 Alternatively, in our conversations with several experts, they suggested that the focus on self-regulation and executive function skills may actually be overstated. They argue that the attention these developmental skills receive in practice may simply be due to the research attention it has received in more recent years. However, much of the literature does suggests that self-regulation is central to school achievement and is a marker of adaptive development (e.g., Blair, 2002; Blair & Razza, 2007; Morrison, Ponitz, & McClelland,

2010), a perspective that was supported by interviews with early childhood practitioners and research on the perspectives of kindergarten teachers (Foulks & Morrow, 1989; McClelland, Morrison, & Holmes, 2000; Rimm-Kaufman, Pianta, & Cox, 2000).
222 Morrison et al. (2010).
223 Center on the Developing Child (2011).
224 Eisenberg & Fabes (1992).
225 Diamond & Lee (2011); Moffitt et al. (2011).
226 Caspi, Henry, McGee, Moffitt, & Silva (1995); Liu (2004).

different thoughts, beliefs, and feelings than the self does, and that those beliefs and desires lead people toward particular actions.[227] As children's general understanding of other people advances, so does their relationship with other children. They acquire the ability to interact with multiple peers, often while engaging in pretend play.

The social interactions that preschool children have with peers lay the groundwork for learning an array of skills that will be necessary for successful social interactions when they are older. For example, play not only requires but also helps to support all kinds of critical aspects of self-regulation, including attentional, behavioral, social, emotional, and cognitive regulation.[228] The back-and-forth communications that young children engage in during play help children learn how to take turns and listen (inhibiting their own desire to interrupt), begin to understand their own feelings and beliefs and those of others, and understand that those different feelings and beliefs influence the behaviors of each individual. Early interactions with peers (and the support young children get from adults in successfully negotiating these interactions) help to shape how children interpret the world (e.g., thinking that people are pleasant or hostile).[229] And as children get better at understanding their peers, they begin to develop a sense of self-efficacy about their ability to be socially engaged.[230] Thus, the origins of some of the mindsets (e.g., openness, self-efficacy) that are crucial during the transition from adolescence into young adulthood seem to first emerge in young children's interactions with peers. Early social and emotional development, accompanied by supportive interactions with adults, produces the earliest signs that children can distinguish *"right"* from *"wrong"*; having these emotional and cognitive abilities

to distinguish between the two and act on that knowledge can be considered some of the earliest foundations of morality—an important component of the values that a young adult will ultimately embrace.

How Do Experiences Shape Development in Early Childhood?

Nothing about early childhood development can be thought of as existing in a vacuum. A reciprocal influential nature exists between the rapid neurological development that infants and young children experience and their opportunities for interactions. These opportunities are in turn shaped by several layers of children's ecosystem,[231] including the immediate environment in which they interact and learn (their parents, peers, early education program) and larger ecosystems that may include local politics, social services, and even larger attitudes, values, and beliefs of the culture they live within.

The most crucial way adults provide supports for a young child is by being consistently responsive to that child's needs.[232] This enables children to feel secure so that they can comfortably explore new facets of their world. Children with secure attachments will reference the adults around them during their preschool years to gain feedback on whether their emotional or behavioral reactions are appropriate in a given context. One aspect of adult-child interactions that are especially important in the early years is language. Being exposed to linguistically-rich interactions helps support the development of a child's own language and ultimately their overall development. However, there are great disparities in how much language young children hear from their caregivers.[233] Children from low-income families hear as many as 30 million words fewer than their higher-income peers[234] and these differences are related to differences in early language development.[235]

---

227 Wellman, Cross, & Watson (2001).
228 Berk, Mann, & Ogan (2006); Bodrova, Germeroth, & Leong (2013).
229 National Research Council and Institute of Medicine (2000).
230 Harter (1982); Ladd and Price (1986).
231 Bronfenbrenner (1979).

232 Bowlby (1982).
233 Hart & Risley (1995).
234 Hart & Risley (1995).
235 Hoff (2003); Huttenlocher, Waterfall, Vasilyeva, Vevea, & Hedges (2010); Rowe (2008).

Children's own language development, in turn, influences a variety of other areas of development, including children's ability to recognize, understand, and manage emotions and behaviors. Between the ages of two and five, several lines of research suggest that language development is a critical component of developing and understanding thought and emotions [236] and self-regulation of emotions.[237] Recent work suggests that targeted interventions with parents can help create a more language-rich environment for their young children.[238]

Conditions created by poverty and inequality—particularly neglect and toxic stress—have an especially large impact on early neurological development, potentially producing lasting challenges to be overcome, such as a child's later ability to succeed in educational or learning activities.[239] Specifically, traumatic experiences in childhood can lead to an over-development of the midbrain and brainstem, producing hyper-reactive and aggressive behaviors.[240] Alternatively, neglect can lead to an under-development of the limbic and cortical regions, which can cause difficulty in cognitive processing.[241] Together, trauma and neglect represent a toxic combination for young people, associated with lower levels of self-regulation and social-emotional skills in later years. Especially when working with underserved children, adults need to create spaces and experiences that are both safe and cognitively stimulating.

Adults best meet children's needs when these contextual factors are taken into account. Barbara Abel, the early childhood curriculum manager at Educare Chicago introduced earlier in the report, describes this nuance in working on self-regulatory processes with young children, many of whom come from very impoverished backgrounds:

You know that day when you oversleep and you wake up and you're an hour late for an important meeting or it's your first day at work on a new job and you realize that you've overslept? What do you feel like? Dysregulated kids feel like that much of the time. So imagine, with your adrenaline constantly flowing, your cortisol levels elevated, with your heart beating a little too fast, not knowing which way to turn—how do you expect someone to learn? And so if some children have all these factors that can compromise their capacity to self-regulate, then we have to look at classrooms and we have to say, 'How do we create a place that makes all the children feel safe so that they can attend?'—Barbara Abel, curriculum manager, Educare Chicago[242]

Indeed, laying the groundwork for positive development in future years requires careful and intentional support from adults, but also recognition that young children have a great number of capabilities. Decades of research in developmental psychology support the notion that even children as young as three years old benefit from the types of developmental experiences and developmental relationships laid out in Chapter 2. Adults can provide children with varied experiences and options for how they would like to spend their time, which encourages children's love for exploration and learning. Providing limits to opportunities, likewise, helps young children grow to respect boundaries and exercise self-regulation. They need experiences that allow them to *"tinker"* or experiment and they benefit from positive role models. Young children flourish when they have adults in their lives who help them put

236 Luria (1961); Vygotsky (1962).
237 Cole, Armstrong, & Pemberton (2010).
238 Leffel & Suskind (2013).
239 Shonkoff et al. (2012).
240 Perry (2006).
241 Perry (2006).
242 UChicago CCSR interview with Barbara Abel, curriculum manager, Educare Chicago (April 21, 2014).

62

language to their experiences and link what they are learning to things they already know (*"connecting"*). For example, high quality preschool classrooms are structured in ways that allow children to make many of their own choices, such as which center they want to spend their time in during free play. They can feed the interest they are having in the moment and, with support from teachers, can *"tinker"* with all sorts of objects. Effective teachers do not tell children explicitly how to make something work; rather they let children explore, experiment, and fail, and then help them make sense out of that failure so they can try something again, ultimately achieving what they set out to do.

How Is Development in Early Childhood Related to Development in Other Stages?

The benefits of investing in early development have become increasingly clear in recent decades; long-term studies following high-risk children who attended high-quality early education programs show great advantages for them compared to similar children who did not attend such programs.[243] Economic models estimating returns on investment show that early childhood programs (birth through preschool) have a larger rate of return than programs implemented at any other point during the life cycle.[244] James Heckman and his colleagues have attempted to understand the ways in which early interventions lead to greater adult outcomes; they find that it is not an increase in IQ, but rather the development of noncognitive factors that accounts for most of the positive effects.[245] Children who attended the Perry Preschool, who were the basis for this analysis, spent a considerable amount of time learning social skills and self-control (i.e., interpersonal knowledge and skills, and self-regulation)—the two primary developmental tasks highlighted here.

The links between early development and later development suggest that a focus on early interpersonal skills and self-regulation can help set children on a positive course of development, whether it is in an academic setting, in their social lives, or at home. Through the use of scaffolding—or supporting children in their current stage of development in preparation for the next stage—adults can help structure the environment for young children so they can gradually learn how to plan, focus their attention, and achieve goals with fewer and fewer supports.[246, 247]

Middle Childhood
(Elementary School-Aged Children; Ages 6 to 10)

Children in elementary school, ages 6 to 10, are in the developmental stage known as *"middle childhood."* This represents a period during which children establish a growing sense of competence, independence, and self-awareness upon which later identity development will build.[248] The changes children experience during this stage are driven by three factors: increased cognitive advances that allow for greater and more abstract thinking, self-regulation, and reflection; social changes that reflect an expanding set of relationships with both adults and peers; and institutional changes that expose children to comparison and competition across multiple domains (e.g., social relationships and academic achievement).[249] These cognitive, social, and institutional changes define the substantial, if often underappreciated, challenge of middle childhood: learning how to navigate multiple contexts in transition while establishing a more stable sense of self.

243 For example, Schweinhart, Montie, Xiang, Barnett, Belfield, & Nores (2005); Campbell & Ramey (1995).
244 Heckman (2008).
245 Heckman, Pinto, & Savelyey (2013).
246 While early childhood is a critical period of development, it is also a difficult time in which to identify those who may need intervention. Children develop at very different rates, and because so much of what is changing in the early childhood years requires maturation of the brain, it is easy to misdiagnose a child as having behavior problems when he is simply physiologically behind. This is an especially precarious time to make strong statements about which children will need severe interventions and which ones just need a bit more scaffolding in early stages of regulatory development (National Research Council and Institute of Medicine, 2000; K. Magnuson, personal communication, June 4, 2014).
247 Center on the Developing Child (2011).
248 Eccles (1999).
249 Eccles (1999).

63

Key Questions

What Internal or External Changes Are Taking Place that Influence Development in Middle Childhood?

Cognitively, children in middle childhood develop and refine the ability to think in increasingly abstract ways, including the capacity for systematically handling more complex representational ideas.[250] In early childhood, children may be able to perform simple tasks that require the coordination of one or two discrete ideas; the ability to think abstractly and systematically about things that are not immediately present begins to develop around ages 6 to 7, culminating in children's ability to understand the logic of concrete objects and events.[251] This ability to understand concepts more theoretically helps to grow children's understanding of themselves; during this stage, they expand the ways in which they understand who they are to include more psychological aspects of themselves, including their capabilities and emotional states.[252]

Children frequently make multiple institutional transitions during middle childhood, including the entry into formal education (elementary school) around age six. This transition presents children of this age range with a new challenge: the need to regulate their behavior *across different settings*. As they enter a formal school setting for the first time, children face new expectations that they adapt their behavior appropriately for this new setting—a setting that could be very unlike other places they have experienced. One of our interviewees, Sara Rimm-Kaufman, a researcher at the University of Virginia who focuses on applied work, describes the kinds of changes children face in this new setting:

> We asked over 3,000 kindergarten teachers from around the country about what they, as teachers, see as the most critical skills for students to have when they make the transition into school. Our initial hunch was that teachers would talk about the importance of early reading skills or other academic competencies. Instead, most teachers deemed following directions as the skill that they believed was the most important. Consider the nature of activities in kindergarten—students need to listen to their teachers, engage in self-directed and small group work, get into line, make transitions between activities. Engaging in any of these activities successfully requires self-regulatory abilities. —Sara Rimm-Kaufman, professor of education, Curry School of Education, University of Virginia[253]

As Rimm-Kaufman describes, children are challenged in many new ways as they enter formal schooling environments, and are expected to exhibit extensive self-regulation in ways they were never expected to before. At the same time, children have increasing exposure to peers and other (nonfamilial) adults, and decreased time spent with families. Thus, while children in the elementary grades are learning to manage their behaviors, they are also using interpersonal skills to negotiate new friendships and managing increasingly independent interactions with peers.

What Are the Primary Areas of Development in Middle Childhood?

As with younger children, those in middle childhood are continuing to develop their self-regulation and interpersonal knowledge and skills. On top of that, there is a large emphasis on developing learning-related, or academic, knowledge and skills (**see Figure 6**).

Self-Regulation: Self-awareness and self-control.
Children's cognitive development is evident not only in advances in their formal reasoning, but also in their capacity for self-reflection—in both academic and social settings. During these years, brain development allows children to hold onto more information at a single point in time and to

---

250 National Research Council (1984).
251 Piaget (1952; 1946/1951; 1970).
252 Rote & Smetana (2014).

253 UChicago CCSR interview with Sara Rimm-Kaufman, professor of education, Curry School of Education, University of Virginia (May 22, 2014).

64

FIGURE 6
Middle Childhood (Elementary School, Ages 6-10)

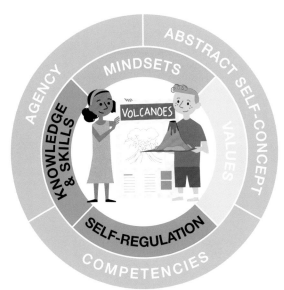

reflect on internal and external stimuli as they become less egocentric.[254, 255] In fact, children's abilities to engage in all aspects of self-regulation expand—in perceiving stimuli, planning, managing, and reflecting. The further development of executive function skills and more abstract thinking enables greater awareness and meaning-making in the increasingly social settings in which they spend time.

General cognitive developments also support another type of awareness during middle childhood: metacognitive awareness—that is, thinking about one's own thought processes. Metacognition allows children to reflect on and adapt their use of concrete, specific learning skills and strategies (e.g., study habits).[256] With the start of formal education, middle childhood is an especially important time for parents and educators to be thinking about ways to develop children's self-regulatory skills, including various types of awareness; these skills underlie many of the behaviors and attributes that are associated with successful school adjustment,[257] a predecessor to continued success in school.

The aforementioned growth in self-regulation and metacognitive abilities has ramifications for strengthening learning-related skills. When children enact learning-related skills, they exhibit behaviors like self-control, staying on task, organizing work materials, working independently, listening and following directions, and participating appropriately in groups.[258] As children progress through middle childhood, the ability to plan, evaluate, and modify their use of strategic learning behaviors develops further. This improvement in learning-related skills helps to support the influx of new knowledge obtained during these years. And indeed, a primary focus within elementary schools—particularly in the earlier grades—is on the acquisition of the content knowledge needed to succeed academically in future years. There are good reasons for this emphasis. First, this is a time period when children's cognitive abilities expand and allow for more effective learning and increased understanding of more complex concepts. Second, when children do not acquire early content knowledge, they are likely to fall behind their peers academically; this follows children throughout the elementary school years and beyond.[259]

Interpersonal skills. Middle childhood is a time when children spend increasing amounts of time with other children, and their growing cognitive capabilities combine with these new experiences to help strengthen their interpersonal skills. Children's growing capacity for self-reflection also manifests in increasingly complex perspective-taking, whereby children become able to handle others' perspectives and to coordinate multiple social categories.[260] Adult support is vital to helping children build healthy peer relationships and negotiating these new tasks; the ability to develop positive friendships with peers through the use of interpersonal skills and behaviors will facilitate positive outcomes later in life. Conversely, the devel-

65

---

254 The term *"egocentric"* is commonly used in the development literature, as it marks a transition from children seeing the world and themselves from their own perspective to seeing them from multiple perspectives.

255 Markus & Nurius (1984).

256 Eccles (1999).

257 Blair (2002).

258 McClelland, Acock, & Morrison (2006).

259 e.g., Clotfelter, Ladd, & Vigdor (2009); Fryer & Levitt (2006).

260 Flavell (1977); Watson (1981).

opment of poor relationships during this period puts children at risk for emotional and behavioral issues in adolescence and in adulthood.[261] For those children who struggle with peer acceptance, there is also an increased likelihood in adolescence of dropping out of school and encounters with police.[262]

How Do Experiences Shape Development in Middle Childhood?

As the increase in cognitive function facilitates an increase in self-reflection and perspective-taking, children begin making sophisticated social comparisons, including comparing and contrasting their own behavior with that of their peers.[263] A supportive environment is vital to the development of a child's self-concept, and in middle childhood, a child's sense of self becomes both more stable and more abstract.[264] There is a great emphasis on the need for developing a strong sense of oneself as capable and independent. As children gain the capacity to compare themselves to others, it is notable that children are likely to think about themselves in a manner that highlights the way they are different or how they stand out from others.[265] They use this information to evaluate themselves as being good at something or not; as such, they begin to develop early mindsets related to self-efficacy and the roles that ability and intelligence play in performing well.[266] While middle childhood remains an important period for developing greater independence, children still rely substantially on adults and institutional settings to provide consistent structure and feedback on their performance, thereby exerting substantial influence on the judgments children reach about themselves, their peers, and their developing identity.

Many of the components articulated in the Foundations for Young Adult Success developmental framework begin or continue to develop in middle childhood, laying the foundation for later success. Our review of the literature indicates a heavy emphasis on cognitive development during these years; indeed, practice—

especially in schools—often hones in on cognitive development and content knowledge. However, a deeper look expands this perspective and highlights that several other foundational components are maturing during this stage of life as well. These include self-regulatory processes; knowledge and skills beyond content knowledge, including learning and social skills; and early mindsets about a person's capabilities to accomplish their aspirations. As adults consider the range of developmental experiences and interactions they provide for elementary school-aged children, it would behoove them to consider the varied needs of youth in this age group.

While the current literature on this developmental stage does examine children in new social situations, the focus is primarily on children in the context of the classroom. In particular, researchers have made great strides recently in identifying the ways self-regulation in middle childhood is associated with adaptive classroom behaviors, the ways and means by which children form friendships based in the classroom during middle childhood, and the ways in which middle childhood is a time of cognitive development. However, less research has focused on children in family and community contexts; the goal of very little research has been to understand how the cognitive, social, emotional, and physical development that occurs during middle childhood happens in the multiple domains of the child's life. Such research is undoubtedly needed, since middle childhood is a time where many different aspects of a child's development must fall into place to support the rapid growth and development that will occur in adolescence.

How Is Development In Middle Childhood Related to Development in Other Stages?

Development in middle childhood builds directly off of the advances children make in early childhood. As children transition from early childhood into middle childhood, their cognitive capabilities continue to expand greatly. The general cognitive changes that take place enable children to think more abstractly, rather

261 National Research Council (1984).
262 Kupersmidt & Coie (1990); Parker & Asher (1987).
263 Ruble (1983).
264 Bannister & Agnew (1976); Guardo & Bohan (1971); Livesley & Bromley (1973); Montemayor & Eisen (1977); Rosenberg (1979).

265 McGuire, McGuire, Child, & Fujioka (1978); McGuire & Padawer-Singer (1976).
266 Gecas (2003); Stipek & Gralinski (1996); Zimmerman & Ringle (1981).

66

than in very concrete ways. This includes a child's sense of self. For example, most children in middle childhood view their self-identity as stable, and do not believe they can become a completely different person.[267] Although frequently conceptualized as a developmental plateau by earlier theorists (e.g., Freud, Piaget), middle childhood represents a critical transitional period during which children establish a growing sense of competence, independence, and self-awareness upon which later identity development during adolescence builds.[268]

A reliance on self-regulation also continues to be crucial in the middle childhood years. As children get older, however, the manifestations of self-regulation begin to change from what they once were. In early childhood, self-regulation largely focuses on the management of emotions and of interactions with peers. As children progress through middle childhood, the goals of self-regulation become broader. They expand to include how to set goals and develop organizational skills, such as remembering to bring a textbook home from school to complete homework. This transition into more advanced types of self-regulation sets the stage for early adolescence when more responsibilities are placed on youth.

Early Adolescence
(Middle School-Aged Children; Ages 11 to 14)

The middle grades roughly overlap with the period of development known as *"early adolescence,"* between ages 11 to 14. This developmental phase is a time of great physiological, psychological, and social change, including entrance into puberty. Also occurring during this period are drastic changes and reorganization in the brain, particularly in the prefrontal cortex, resulting in significant cognitive developments.[269] Early adolescents begin to capitalize on their previous knowledge, skills, and self-regulatory abilities to build toward high-level thinking and more coordinated social activities. They show marked improvements in their deductive reasoning, cognitive flexibility, efficiency and capacity for information processing, and expertise in a variety of domains,[270] including *"improvements in various aspects of executive functioning, including long-term planning, metacognition, self-evaluation, self-regulation, and the co-ordination of affect and cognition."*[271] Kelly Dwyer, chief knowledge officer of Spark, an out-of-school program for middle school students, describes the plethora of changes taking place for youth of this age:

> Middle school is such an intense time period for kids; they're growing older in every way you could possibly grow, and they bring that to everything they do...First of all, in their prefrontal cortex all these synapses from childhood get pruned away—things that they're not really using as much—and the synapses that are in their brain start to become more solid...And then also in their limbic system, their hormones are basically like lighting that up, right? And that system is in charge of how a person assesses risk and how willing they are to take risk...The other big thing is, from a personality development standpoint, they're thinking about who they are in the world for the first time. —Kelly Dwyer, chief knowledge officer, Spark[272]

Amidst these changes, literature has identified the major developmental task during adolescence as the search for identity.[273]

Key Questions

What Internal or External Changes Are Taking Place that Influence Development in Early Adolescence? Since the foundational components and the key factors for young adult success can only be developed through interactions with others, or psychological reciprocity, young people in this stage will seek a peer group to help advance their development.[274] In particular, early adolescents are using peers to explore some sort of identity.

267 Guardo & Bohan (1971).
268 Eccles (1999).
269 Blakemore & Choudhry (2006).
270 Blakemore & Choudhry (2006).
271 Steinberg (2005, p. 70).
272 UChicago CCSR interview with Kelly Dwyer, chief knowledge officer, Spark (April 25, 2014).
273 Erikson (1950/1963).
274 Erikson (1950/1963).

The peer social context becomes much more influential during this stage of life, and young adolescents are preoccupied with trying to find where they fit. The increased executive function skills and awareness also enable an acute attention to social status among peers.

As with youth in middle childhood, early adolescents enter a very different institutional environment as they move from elementary school into middle school and/or the start of high school. Overall, early adolescence represents a great time of change, and young people's experiences during this period can set them on a trajectory that will continue to influence their development through middle adolescence and young adulthood.

What Are the Primary Areas of Development in Early Adolescence?

Youth in early adolescence continue to develop their self-regulation and interpersonal knowledge and skills, but the most salient areas of development during these years are group-based identity development and a number of mindsets (**see Figure 7**).

Group-based identity development. As young teens enter the middle grades, they are very concerned with *"developing a sense of group cohesion"* with peers,[275] much more so than in previous stages. The peer group affiliation drives development of foundational components such as mindsets and an awareness of self, as well as values derived from their peer group. Teens *"look to their peers for acceptance, importance, and unity. Within the context of building peer relations, adolescents learn loyalty, empathy, criticism, and rejection."*[276] The sense of belonging they seek shapes adolescents' early identity, particularly their social identity as being autonomous from their parents and family. During this time, youth are learning to establish more intimate friendships and staking out some degree of independence from their parents and families by identifying with a crowd. This identification provides clear developmental

FIGURE 7

Early Adolescence (Middle Grades, Ages 11-14)

benefits and influences on early adolescents: crowds contribute to identity development by connecting teens to a social network and establishing norms of behavior for their members.[277] These changes help adolescents build narratives of themselves separate from their family unit, and apply agency toward new interests outside of the home.

Emerging mindsets. As young teens seek out peers who dress, look, and behave like they do to find acceptance in a peer group[278] (and simultaneously change their dress, look, and behavior to fit in), a number of mindsets are being developed. Here, the onset of puberty and the development of sexuality during early adolescence add complexity to social bonds with same-age peers. Any physical features that seem to differentiate one from the crowd have a considerable impact on a middle school student's view of self, and even a negative psychological impact.[279] In particular, the focus on peer acceptance affects young adolescents' self-efficacy and self-esteem.[280] As they enter early adolescence,

275 Hazen, Scholzman, & Beresin (2008, p. 163).
276 Gutgesell & Payne (2004, p. 80).
277 Susman et al. (1994).
278 Akers, Jones, & Coyl (1998); Gutgesell & Payne (2004); Hogue & Steinberg (1995).
279 Gutgesell & Payne (2004); Hazen, Scholzman, & Beresin (2008).

280 Self-esteem refers to the general valuing of one's worth. Whereas self-concept describes the content of the self, self-esteem places a value on that content and is thus associated with positive (pride) or negative (shame, disgust) emotions that coincide with a positive or negative judgment.

teens experience more day-by-day fluctuations in self-esteem than they did in childhood, though these eventually stabilize over time.[281] Important influences on self-esteem in adolescence include parental approval, peer support, adjustment, and success in school.[282] When early adolescents have greater self-esteem, they are more likely to feel a sense of self-efficacy about different activities and relationships they are engaged in.

As youth transition into the middle grades in early adolescence, a change in academic attributions also occurs. Recall that in middle childhood, children begin to sense that they are *"good"* or *"not good"* at something; in early adolescence, this materializes into a more articulated distinction between ability and effort, or *"not working hard enough"* and *"not being smart enough."*[283] Over time, young teens begin to develop a *"fixed"* mindset (as opposed to a growth mindset); that is, they tend to attribute performance increasingly to ability, or at least to see ability as a more formidable constraint on their performance.[284] These emerging mindsets have implications for students' success as they navigate the transition into high school. For a significant number of students, their performance attributions, coupled with their doubts about the malleability of intelligence, cause them to withdraw effort just when the academic context requires both more effort and better use of appropriate strategies for learning. The emphasis on social comparison in the middle grades also sets up a context in which less prepared or lower performing students do not want to call attention to their learning struggles and *"may adopt behaviors and strategies to avoid failures—devaluing challenging tasks, self-handicapping, and withdrawing effort altogether."*[285]

How Do Experiences Shape Development in Early Adolescence?

The fact that early adolescents are grappling with these new ways of seeing themselves—in terms of both identity and self-efficacy—has implications for how they react to the school settings in which they spend much of their time. Jacqueline Eccles and her colleagues have shown how cognitive and social behavior changes in early adolescence collided with school environments and instructional practices in a way that undermined students' engagement and performance; in essence, they described a lack of *"fit"* between early adolescents' developmental stage and the middle school environment.[286] These findings are summarized in an earlier UChicago CCSR report:

> Paradoxically, at a time when adolescents are becoming developmentally ready to assert increasing personal autonomy and assume greater responsibility for their learning, middle grades classrooms become more (not less) restrictive, placing greater emphasis on teacher control and diminishing opportunities for student choice and independence. Second, at a time when early adolescents become increasingly sensitive to social comparison, instructional practices in middle grades classrooms tend to reward ability over effort and highlight social comparison. Third, at a time when adolescents develop the ability to engage in more complex, abstract forms of problem-solving, the academic demand of class assignments declines during the middle grades—schoolwork often becomes less (not more) challenging.[287]

69

---

281 Alasker & Olweus (1992).
282 DuBois, Bull, Sherman, & Roberts (1998); Luster & McAdoo (1995); Steinberg & Morris (2001).
283 Nicholls & Miller (1984).
284 Covington (1984); Dweck & Leggett (1988); Nicholls & Miller (1984).
285 Farrington et al. (2012, p. 56).
286 Eccles, Lord, & Midgley (1991); Eccles & Midgley (1989); Eccles, Midgley, & Adler (1984).
287 Farrington et al. (2012, p. 57).

Creating successful contexts for early adolescents—whether inside or outside of schools—would require that we meet their developmental needs for increasing independence from adult control, extended interaction with peers, exploration with things they have interest in, and opportunities to engage in increasingly complex forms of thinking, communicating, and problem-solving. It also calls for attending to the various foundational components that are in play during every experience an adolescent has. One example of a program that is helping to support youth in these ways is Spark, an out-of-school apprenticeship program that works with middle grade students to address the issue of disengagement that occurs in middle school. Their executive director of Spark, Chicago describes:

> Students in middle grades don't find a direct link between what they're doing in school and their life. Classroom learning is not tied to their personal interests and it's not hands-on. So they're bored by the way they're learning... Spark is trying to make those connections for students. One example is a student, Jeffrey, who was struggling in math but loves to skateboard. We paired him with a mentor at an architecture firm for his apprenticeship. For his Spark project, he actually got to build a skate park because, of course, that ties to his interests, and he was super excited. But then, Jeffrey starts to understand why geometry is important and how he might relate math to something that he likes and is interested in. —Kathleen St. Louis Caliento, executive director, Spark, Chicago[288]

This example highlights how developmental experiences—in this case, in-school learning vs. an apprenticeship aligned to Jeffrey's interests—can either hinder or facilitate youth engagement with exploration and learning. Indeed, scholars have argued that the more rigid structure, decreased individual attention, and evaluative environment of middle and high schools constitute a mismatch between developmental stage and the environment, which exacerbates many problem behaviors.[289] By attending to Jeffrey's interests and adapting his experiences to those interests that he holds (a key aspect of developmental relationships), Jeffrey is more likely to engage in learning; the experiences presented to him support a higher level of connection between his apprenticeship and school, and thus an expansion of his existing skills.

How Is Development in Early Adolescence Related to Development in Other Stages?

As the focus moves from middle childhood to early adolescence, there is a distinct shift in the literature from an emphasis on the development of self-regulation and early social interactions toward the development of identities—particularly adolescents' social and academic identities. During these early adolescent ages, youth are continuing to develop abstract thinking and focusing more on the comparison of the self to others. These developments allow for further refinement of self-awareness and executive function skills, including self-regulation, metacognition, setting goals for oneself, and the application of learned strategies, all of which support the achievement of academic, social, and personal success. Youth in early adolescence are also laying the groundwork for later identity development, particularly the various identities and opportunities for agency that will emerge in different parts of their lives as they move into their later teen years.

In short, the middle grades may be best understood as a time of intense transition as young teens begin to pull away from family and seek to establish themselves in the world of their peers, grappling with the meaning of the self in relation to others. As researchers Gutgesell and Payne observe, *"the teen is finding self-expression and forming moral thought while struggling with an emerging image of self in society."* [290] Peers clearly have a powerful, ongoing influence on early adolescents' conceptions of themselves, their psychological development, and their daily behaviors, all of which contribute to their emerging senses of identities.

---

288 UChicago CCSR interview with Kathleen St. Louis Caliento, executive director, Spark, Chicago (February 13, 2014).

289 Eccles et al. (1993); Halpern, Heckman, & Larson (2013).
290 Gutgesell & Payne (2004, p. 80).

Middle Adolescence
(High School-Aged Youth; Ages 15 to 18)

Youth in high school, roughly ages 15 to 18, are in what is known as middle adolescence, the developmental stage that follows the drastic physical and neurological changes of puberty. Middle adolescence brings more physiological stability and better adjustment—psychological and social—to the changes that occurred during the previous stage of adolescence. However, this is also a time associated with greater risk-taking and experimentation as adolescents advance their various senses of identity and agency. In fact, the fundamental developmental task in this stage is for teenagers to sample widely the broad range of roles and experiences available to them, while not jeopardizing long-term health and safety.

Key Questions

What Internal or External Changes Are Taking Place that Influence Development in Middle Adolescence?

Several factors support greater identity formation in the high school years, including continued increases in cognitive capacity and changes in adolescents' social relationships. Entrance to high school brings with it a wide variety of new opportunities and experiences, as well as increased academic demands. Though not all teens engage in or have opportunities for all experiences, it is during this developmental stage that young people generally begin dating and entering into sexual relationships, driving a car (opening up new opportunities for independence), working in paid employment, and experimenting with drugs and alcohol; each of these experiences contributes to further development of various identities in the multiple facets of their lives (e.g., as a romantic partner, as an employee). Middle adolescents also begin having to make decisions with both high-stakes and long-term consequences.

Cognitive developments during this phase support teenagers' ability to appreciate, learn from, and value different viewpoints. The thinking of teens in the high school years is less confined to absolutes (black and white), giving them a higher level of comfort with ambiguity. This corresponds with a greater acceptance of others' individuality and less emphasis on conformity to group norms that characterized their social relationships in early adolescence.[291] Their cliques expand to include peers of the opposite sex, and they spend increasing amounts of time in mixed-sex groups.[292] High school-aged adolescents also tend to have somewhat broader and/or more numerous social groups than they had in the middle grades, and they are more willing to step out of their comfort zone to experiment with different aspects of the self.

What Are the Primary Areas of Development in Middle Adolescence?

During the high school years, the major developmental tasks include discovering a sense of values and an individuated identity (**see Figure 8**). These rely on developing positive mindsets and knowledge of the self that is differentiated from others.

Values. In contrast to earlier stages, having a sense of personal values emerges as a self-defining characteristic for middle adolescents. Whereas young children define themselves in terms of concrete attributes and middle-schoolers define themselves by a peer group, high school-aged youth form a much more independent sense of the things they place value in. Teenagers in this age range experience a higher level of cognitive functioning, which gives them greater capacity to identify and reflect on what they value about themselves, their peers and family members, and the world writ-large. They *"begin to view themselves in terms of personal beliefs and standards, and less in terms of social comparisons."*[293] This is important for future endeavors because when an individual determines what holds value, he is more motivated to harness his knowledge and skills toward that end; in this way, values play a crucial role in exercising agency toward realizing one's potential. Additionally,

71

---

291 Shulman, Laursen, Kalman, & Karpovsky (1997).
292 Brown (1990).

293 Steinberg & Morris (2001, p. 91), with additional reference to Harter (1998).

establishing a clear set of individual values can help link past experiences with current and future motivations and behaviors, and thus will be central in forming an integrated identity.[294]

Individuated identity. In contrast with early adolescence, when youth define themselves by the norms and interests of their peer groups, middle adolescents begin asking *"big questions"* about themselves, their values, and their place in the world.[295] They are seeking an individuated identity—a sense of who they are independent of others around them. Young people in this age range *"are beginning to find their own voice, beliefs, and values; and they are beginning to set and act on personal goals. They are learning to invest in their own learning experiences, productivity, and creativity; and they are forging the enduring motivational structures that will carry them into adulthood."*[296] These developments play a crucial role in how youth begin to define their individuated identities, and ultimately how well they are able to consolidate their various *"selves"* into an integrated identity.

FIGURE 8
Middle Adolescence (High School, Ages 15-18)

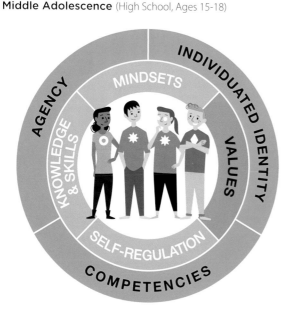

How Do Experiences Shape Development in Middle Adolescence?

Neurological changes during middle adolescence lead to lower levels of self-regulation, resulting in a time of increased risk-taking. Some adolescents are wired to seek pleasure and excitement without the benefit of adequate compensatory regulatory control. As Lawrence Steinberg described it, there is a mismatch between *"the gas pedal and the brake."* Particularly in the early years of high school, there is an increase in the activity and development of the areas of the brain associated with pleasure-seeking and rewards, while development in the areas of the brain associated with behavior regulation is not complete until later in life.[297] Combine this developmental mismatch with adolescents' search for individuated identity and this stage of life becomes a time when many teens experiment and put themselves in new situations to try out various potential *"selves."* These experiences provide the essential raw material from which they will be able to form a more mature integrated identity. In all these cases, the experience of trying on new roles, exploring the self, and considering one's place amongst others drives identity integration. Lila Leff, founder of Umoja Student Development Corporation, encapsulates how natural it is for adolescents to tinker, practice, and choose different roles:

> I think one important part of building out an identity is that you practice and play around in things and think about who you want to be in them. And you try on different roles. Think about all the different personalities you can take on when you're babysitting, or you're working at the movie theater with kids you don't go to school with, or you're doing whatever. Kids need time and room to do that and to figure out: How do I see myself? Can I still be true to myself and

---

294 Côté (2009).
295 Halpern, Heckman, & Larson (2013).
296 Halpern, Heckman, & Larson (2013, p. 8).
297 Casey, Getz, & Galvin (2008); Steinberg (2007).

talk differently in different situations? It's practicing code switching; not because somebody told it to you, but because you really experienced it. —Lila Leff, founder, Umoja Student Development Corporation[298]

As a practitioner, it can sometimes be difficult to distinguish between harmless experimentation and *"enduring patterns of dangerous and troublesome behavior."*[299] Many adolescents exhibit a pattern of problem behaviors that are adolescence-limited and developmentally normative.[300] It turns out that most serious problems observed in middle adolescence actually had their start at an earlier age. Accordingly, predicting long-term behavioral problems is best assessed by looking at behaviors *before* entry to adolescence, which places additional importance on monitoring social-emotional behaviors in middle childhood. Most problems that present themselves for the first time in adolescence are *"relatively transitory in nature and are resolved by the beginning of adulthood, with few long-term repercussions."*[301]

Like the mismatch between early adolescents and middle schools described in the previous section, we see evidence of a similar lack of fit between the developmental needs of older adolescents and many high schools. Studies often find that adolescent students exhibit decreased interest and motivation to learn and seem unwilling to take on the challenging academic tasks of high school.[302] Researchers Halpern, Heckman, and Larson argue that this is largely because high schools afford young people *"little opportunity to experience a sense of ownership [or] deepening participation in a goal-oriented community"*[303] aligned with their developing capacities and interests. When students enter high school, they experience a decline in emotional support for learning from teachers and peers,[304] along with a high-stakes assessment environment that amounts to a *"motivational framework based on fear,"* often resulting in young people's *"intellectual and psychological withdrawal."*[305]

Despite this misalignment, the high school context is one setting that drives the development or reinforcement of foundational components during this period. The knowledge students gain through high school education—particularly the knowledge they gain relative to their peers—will affect future success, both by directly affecting the acquisition of further knowledge and through changes in self-efficacy caused by self-awareness of their relative academic standing. Their ability to overcome self-regulation challenges will inform the extent to which they are able to develop and exhibit important competencies, and high school performance will inform mindsets about the self and the self as a student. In the process of identity development, adolescents need to experiment with new roles and responsibilities and try on new images of the self. They need to be exposed to and explore *"future possible selves"* that they might not have previously imagined for themselves,[306] and these opportunities will be fostered or constrained by the school context they are in.

Middle adolescents need opportunities to generate data about the self in response to the questions that most motivate them: *"Who am I?" "What do I have to offer to others?"* and *"What can I do in the world?"* Without support for this kind of exploration, adolescents in the high school years are not able to fulfill the developmental tasks before them. The challenge is in finding productive outlets and opportunities for their developing capacities, such as opportunities in out-of-school activities, work, and community settings.

How Is Development in Middle Adolescence Related to Development in Other Stages?

Early development of mindsets continues to influence how youth in this stage interact with others and respond to their experiences. It remains crucial that as middle adolescents seek out an understanding of their values and identity, adults encourage youth to be open to new experiences. When adolescents engage with a

298 UChicago CCSR interview with Lila Leff, founder, Umoja Student Development Corporation (January 30, 2014).
299 Steinberg & Morris (2001, p. 86).
300 Moffitt (1993, 2003).
301 Steinberg & Morris (2001, p. 87).
302 Marks (2000); Stipek (2004); Vedder-Weiss & Fortuc (2011).
303 Halpern, Heckman, & Larson (2013, p. 6); see also Certo, Cauley, & Chafin (2003); DeWit, Karioja, & Rye (2010); Smith (2003).
304 DeWit, Karioja, & Rye (2010).
305 Halpern, Heckman, & Larson (2013, p. 7).
306 Oyserman & Fryberg (2006).

wide array of experiences, it lays the groundwork for future decisions post-high school.

High school adolescents recognize seeming discrepancies in the self, and may describe themselves in terms of behavior that can differ according to differing social contexts (for example, being shy at school, gregarious with friends, and respectful toward parents). As teenagers continue to mature, they report fewer such discrepancies and a more consistent view of themselves across contexts.[307] Studies also show that *"adolescents evaluate themselves both globally and along several distinct dimensions—academics, athletics, appearance, social relations, and moral conduct."*[308] The ability to recognize these various *"selves,"* and understand that they can both be distinct from one another and still contribute to a single identity, is the basis for what happens in the next stage of development: developing an integrated identity.

Transitioning into Young Adulthood
(Ages 19 to 22)

Late adolescence is a culmination of all the growth and development that has transpired from birth to this stage. Youth ages 19 to 22 are transitioning from adolescence into young adulthood—a time when individuals begin to make their own decisions about the path they will take as an independent adult. The primary developmental task of young adulthood is integrating different social roles into a coherent identity with a stable set of commitments to roles, values, and beliefs. Compared with early and middle adolescence, young adults show increasing maturity in their selection of and participation in social groups. Whereas early adolescents had a strong drive to belong to same-age social groups to foster their evolving identity, for young adults *"the goal of independence dominates thinking; vocational, educational, and personal issues are major decisions."*[309] Belonging to a *"crowd"* grows continually less important as young people display *"increasing comfort with [their] capacity to choose among many different groups and to endorse*

selectively the values that have particular relevance" to them.[310] Sexual orientation and gender identity become consolidated in middle and young adulthood. The primary social development in young adulthood is the entry into romantic and longer-term sexual relationships. Sexual experimentation is normal and expected.[311]

Throughout the adolescent years, youth are working toward their own notions of identity. By young adulthood, a person with an integrated identity has *"an explicit theory of oneself as a person,"*[312] what Northwestern University professor Dan McAdams calls a *"narrative identity,"* with explanatory power to make the many plot twists of one's life cohere around an organized, singular, and agentic sense of self.[313] To achieve this notion of rational agency requires a process of holistic development: integrating the various domains of one's personhood into one integrated sense of self, with all the parts working in conjunction to achieve one's individual and social purposes.

Primary Area of Development in the Post-High School Years: Integrated Identity

Erik Erikson postulated that the key task of adolescence was to develop a viable sense of identity that links childhood with adulthood and that situates choice and agency within the individual.[314] Adolescents who *"do not form a coherent sense of self and values...will lack a consistent sense of identity as they progress into adulthood."*[315] According to a further articulation of Erikson's theory of identity development espoused by James Marcia, as adolescents get closer to adulthood, they experience more pressure to make choices about their future. Individuals are either able to make commitments to particular values and beliefs and integrate their multiple social roles into their identity, or they adopt a ready-made identity handed to them by others without really considering a wider range of options, or they simply give up on making such commitments and return to a state of identity diffusion.[316]

74

---

307 Harter & Monsour (1992); Harter, Waters, & Whitesell (1998).
308 Steinberg & Morris (2001, p. 91), with additional reference to Masten et al. (1995).
309 Gutgesell & Payne (2004, p. 81).
310 Hazen, Scholzman, & Beresin (2008, p. 163).
311 Gutgesell & Payne (2004); Hazen, Scholzman, & Beresin (2008).

312 Moshman (2005, pp. 89-91).
313 McAdams & Adler (2010).
314 Erikson (1950/1963).
315 Hazen, Scholzman, & Beresin (2008, p. 163).
316 Marcia (1966).

FIGURE 9
Young Adulthood (Post-Secondary, Ages 19-22)

Young adulthood is a critical time period in determining the future of one's life. The process of integrating identity is best supported by exposing young people to a variety of opportunities and possibilities—of roles, perspectives, educational and career paths, and future possible selves—and encouraging them to explore these options, rather than constraining their choices or pushing them to quickly choose a long-term path. Success in the developmental task of this stage rests on the foundation built in earlier stages of life, but it is fundamentally determined by the approach older adolescents take to making choices and commitments for their future. In young adulthood, many youth are continuing to build upon the foundational components depicted in the Developmental Framework for Young Adult Success (**see Figure 9**); they possess stronger reasoning capacities and the ability to anticipate long-term outcomes. They have the ability to set goals with a narrative that helps support their planfulness and select strategies to achieve them. Their cognitive growth also enables young adults to overcome the risk-taking behavior of middle adolescence, and enact better self-regulation over their emotions and behaviors. All of

this depends on a firm footing of the foundational components shown previously: awareness of self and others and self-regulatory control, the knowledge and skills one has developed through school and other learning activities, the mindsets one has cultivated, and the values one is committed to. Finally, though, they depend on the identity choices one makes, and the extent to which those choices are based on a broad sampling of possibilities.

With positive and varied experiences throughout early development, young adults are bound to have the physiological and cognitive capacities they will need to embark on a life that is both independent yet connected to important others. If all has gone well up to that point, or if adults intervened at key points when help was needed, the young adult will most likely be able to integrate her various life experiences, roles, and group memberships into a coherent and autonomous sense of self. The ultimate goal of positive youth development is to support children, adolescents, and young adults to set their own aspirations and have the agency and competencies to attain their goals. As so clearly stated by one of our interviewees who works with adolescents and young adults, Leslie Beller, the goal is to develop youth into individuals who exhibit the following:

> The ability to make active choices over their own future, and make legitimate choices grounded in an understanding of who they are, grounded in an understanding of the social realities which they face, understanding how to actually overcome those barriers if desired, and to feel confident that the choices they make are grounded in their own understanding of themselves and their understanding of their own context, which would allow systems to not manipulate them as [they do] often based on the economic needs. —Leslie Beller, Chicago Public Schools, and director and founder, MHA Labs[317]

75

---

317 UChicago CCSR interview with Leslie Beller, director and founder, MHA Labs (January 29, 2014).

What happens as adolescents transition into young adulthood is strongly shaped by the ways in which and degrees to which earlier developmental tasks were met. They draw upon the foundation laid in each preceding stage or the interventions that have successfully compensated for prior developmental lapses. To meet the development tasks as one embarks on young adulthood, a young person should be able to draw upon a basis of secure attachment/trust; the core components of self-regulation, including awareness and reflection; a sense of their own agency and ability to take initiative; and a robust sense of possibility based on exploration. An integrated identity is best achieved when youth are presented with and encouraged to explore a wide variety of opportunities and life possibilities and develop key competencies before prematurely deciding on one course or inadvertently limiting their options by failing to act. Integrated identity draws on experiences and opportunities, incorporating them into memory to shape future behavior patterns and self-concept.

CHAPTER 4

Conclusion and Implications for Practice, Policy, and Research

In the United States today, youth are coming of age amidst substantial and widening economic inequality, coupled with diminishing access to opportunity for huge segments of the population.

This delivers a *"one-two"* punch for far too many children: they experience the extra burdens of being on the wrong side of the economic divide—food insecurity, unstable housing, exposure to community violence, toxic stress—compounded by stark differences by income, race/ethnicity, and geography in access to high-quality educational opportunities, access to preventative health care, and parental and community investments in experiences that foster learning and growth. Inequality is reproduced in part by limiting young people's opportunities to develop assets that are valued in society. The stark reality is that, whether we think in terms of traditional domains of academic knowledge and skills, *"21st century"* competencies (e.g., problem-solving, critical thinking, and communication), or individual artistic or intellectual passions, young people face clear and significant gaps in opportunity to reach their full potential. This plays out in a number of ways. For example, as payoffs to advanced education are rising,[318] post-secondary opportunities that can lay the groundwork for successful young adulthood are increasingly constrained by gaps in earlier opportunities to develop basic knowledge and skills from early childhood through high school. The sad fact is that, in the United States today, large swaths of the population are denied the opportunities to develop the competencies,

knowledge, skills, and self-regulatory capacities that are essential for productive adult functioning, or the mindsets, values, agency, and integrated identity that would enable them to set and achieve goals of personal importance and direct their own lives.

The good news is that there is a strong convergence of evidence about how young people develop and learn, with a growing number of examples of this knowledge applied in practice. This report draws upon the research, theory, and practice knowledge base from a range of disciplines and approaches, spanning Dewey's theory of learning from nearly a century ago to recent findings from neuroscience on how the brain works, and synthesizes it into an accessible framework designed to guide the efforts of all adults who are responsible for raising, educating, or otherwise working with children and youth. In the past several years, a large number of frameworks and standards have been created to provide guidance on *what* young people need to learn. The Foundations for Young Adult Success developmental framework describes *how* to enact these frameworks and standards. It characterizes the experiences and relationships youth need to develop into young adults who have agency, an integrated identity, and the requisite competencies to successfully meet the complex challenges of young adulthood and become

---

318 Goldin & Katz (2008, 2009).

thriving, contributing members of their communities.

The vision behind the Foundations for Young Adult Success developmental framework is about building a society where all children grow up to reach their full potential regardless of which side of the economic divide they are born on. Currently, opportunities for rich and varied developmental experiences through K-12 schooling and informal education are largely determined by family resources; to address these inequities, it will not be enough to simply expand options by adding more well-run programs, providing a few more resources, or reforming a subset of schools. Expanding and improving options only improves access for the subset of young people who are more motivated or fortunate enough to live nearby; it still leaves many young people behind. More systematic change will be necessary to address the underlying inequities that shape the life chances of young people. It will mean building a collective sense of responsibility for expanding the possibilities for all young people, not just for our own biological children.

It will also take a transformation of adult beliefs and practices within the existing institutions and structures that shape children's learning and development. It means integrating afterschool providers' lens of youth development with educators' knowledge of learning theory with families' deep understanding of the unique needs and circumstances of their children. By drawing from the knowledge, approaches, and experience of many different adults from many different settings, we can give the next generation of young people the opportunities they need to meet their full potential.

The approach described in this report (1) identifies key factors and foundational components of young adult success, (2) considers how the backgrounds of and contexts in which young people live affect their development, (3) uses a developmental lens, and (4) makes the intentional provision of opportunities for young people to experience, interact, and make meaning of their experiences the central vehicle for learning and development. The Foundations for Young Adult Success developmental framework has clear implications for schools, youth organizations, and families, but without larger transformations in the policy landscape and larger societal and economic context, there are limits to what can be achieved. Many questions remain about

how to more effectively support the development of young people and what policies and structural changes are needed; these form the basis for the research agenda needed to guide these transformations. The world we envision for the next generation of young people will require the joint efforts of educators, youth practitioners, parents and families, policymakers, and researchers. In this concluding chapter, we highlight implications for each group.

Implications for Educators, Youth Practitioners, and Parents and Families

A Narrow Focus on Content Knowledge in Isolation from the Other Foundational Components Undermines Learning and Development

Learning and development are holistic processes dependent on interactions among all of the foundational components (self-regulation, knowledge and skills, mindsets, and values). There may be conceptual reasons for distinguishing between *"cognitive"* and *"noncognitive"* factors, but this distinction has no functional meaning. Cognition, emotion, affect, and behavior are reflexive, mutually reinforcing, and inextricably associated with one another as a part of development and learning. Adults will make little headway if they target only one particular component or subcomponent in isolation. A lesson or activity might focus on a particular foundational component or key factor—be it content knowledge, emotion regulation, a growth mindset, interpersonal skills, or self-awareness—but creating an effective developmental experience rests on being intentional about the contributions each component makes to the learning experience and the ways young people are making meaning of that experience. In schools, for example, teachers are not effectively supporting optimal growth and understanding if they attend solely to teaching content knowledge. If the directions in an algebra lesson are unclear, a student may make meaning of this experience by believing that he cannot do algebra, thus undermining his self-efficacy in the class. The student may also decide that algebra does not matter and is not worth any effort, preferring this interpretation to believing he is not capable of doing algebra. In addition, if the teacher does not establish clear routines and expectations for students, the process of self-regulation necessary for learning becomes more complicated. If there are unresolved interpersonal issues among kids in a classroom, their minds might be on their peers rather than on quadratic equations. In short, the task of ensuring that students learn algebra is dependent on every other dimension of learning.

Teachers, youth workers, and parents can ask themselves questions to ensure they are taking a holistic approach to learning. Am I making sure that failure is not punished and that my child is encouraged to take risks and is open to trying new skills? Do youth have multiple chances to improve so they can develop a growth mindset? Am I helping my students develop metacognitive strategies by giving them time to reflect on the steps they took to do a lesson and consider how to improve their performance? Have I provided an opportunity for young people to think about how they might apply this content to things they care about in the world? By intentionally attending to the foundational components, teachers and other adults can guide how young people make meaning and internalize learning experiences.

Taking a Developmental Lens Is Essential to Ensuring That Structures and Practices Meet the Developmental Needs of the Young People Being Served

Although a lot is known about development, too often, there is a mismatch between the structures or practices in a youth setting and the developmental needs of the young people being served. Schools, youth programs, and even families are too often oriented to adult needs and goals (e.g., maintaining classroom discipline) instead of taking a youth-centered approach. For example, during the early and middle adolescent years, school settings become increasingly structured, less social, and less reflective at a time when youth need ample opportunities to engage with each other, explore their varied interests, and have support in evaluating events in relation to who they are and who they want to become.

Adults should have a solid understanding of the developmental needs of the young people they work with and should tailor the developmental experiences and

supports they provide to the age of the youth. Although all aspects of the developmental experiences described in this report are relevant at all stages of childhood and adolescence, they vary considerably in practice depending on children's age and their cognitive and emotional development. For example, a reflective experience might consist of helping a young child understand a hurtful interaction that occurred during free play. By helping that child remember a time when she was in a similar situation, adults can play a crucial role in supporting that child's understanding of others' feelings. For an adolescent, developmental experiences would look more sophisticated and be more closely aligned with a youth's ongoing formation of her identity and vision for who she could be in the future. For example, a teacher might debrief a disciplinary incident with a student, reflecting on how others have solved a similar disagreement, and how the student's actions may or may not align with her values and identity. In either case, the most effective developmental experiences will focus on the foundational components and key factors most malleable and salient in that individual's developmental stage. Taking into consideration differences across age ranges and across individual children is crucial for creating experiences that are developmentally appropriate.[319]

Ensuring All Young People Have Access to a Multitude of Rich Developmental Experiences Is Imperative to Their Success

Growing up in marginalized communities adds to the complexity of developing into a young adult who is poised for success. While having agency equips young people to make choices and take action, their ability to successfully pursue a desired path also depends on social relationships, financial resources, and countless other external factors that are inequitably distributed. Further, the task of *"integrating"* one's identity is vastly more complicated for low-income youth and youth of color than it is for children who grow up within the social and behavioral norms of the dominant white, middle-class culture.[320]

---

319 Bredekamp (1987); Copple & Bredekamp (2009).

320 Deutsch (2008); Fedelina Chávez & Guido-DiBrito (1999); Phinney (1989); Phinney & Rosenthal (1992).

Responding to this reality requires a careful balance of pragmatism and aspiration. The Foundations for Young Adult Success developmental framework is designed to strike a balance between helping youth thrive in the world as it is, and developing the skills and dispositions they need to challenge a profoundly unjust status quo.[321] On one hand, school-based educators, staff in youth development organizations, and parents must prepare children to succeed in the current economy. For example, in addition to good grades and good test scores, young people from marginalized groups often need to learn to decipher and navigate unfamiliar social and institutional norms to access post-secondary opportunities. Adults do a disservice, particularly to underserved youth, if they do not recognize such realities. On the other hand, educators, practitioners, and parents can equip youth with the skills to challenge cultural norms and inequitable distributions of resources that can limit their opportunities and constrain their potential. In addition to laying out how to prepare young people for the world that is, the report provides guidance on some core questions about the world that could be: How can we design and enact practices within schools, youth organizations, families, and communities that inspire young people to not only reach their own potential, but also to create a better world? How can we help youth develop the knowledge, skills, mindsets, competencies, and agency that would enable them to confront injustice and work toward a more inclusive society?

Young people experience events, interact with others, and undergo a constant process of making observations and connections to their prior experiences to help them make meaning. They develop preferences, figure out strategies for managing relationships and determine whether an experience is something they would like to repeat. But if we hope to direct the development of young people toward positive mindsets and values and having self-regulation and skills and knowledge, adults need to structure experiences to enhance positive development and help young people internalize the lessons from these experiences. Ensuring that all young people have access to a multitude of rich devel-

opmental experiences—from early childhood through adolescence—is imperative to helping youth develop the key factors for success in young adulthood and the foundational components that underlie those factors.

Implications for Education and Youth Policy

The Foundations for Young Adult Success developmental framework provides an ambitious vision of how youth-serving adults could think holistically about development and provide rich experiences that allow young people to grow into successful young adults. This is not an endeavor that can be undertaken by heroic adults acting alone; it will require parallel efforts to rethink what policies and structures are needed to provide opportunities to children and youth; support adults who raise, teach, or care for young people; and facilitate coordination and learning across sectors. An understanding of the need for collaboration across settings and agencies to support holistic development of young people has been gaining traction; efforts such as the Strive Network and the Harlem Children's Zone have been spreading across the nation. However, one big obstacle to holistic youth development resides in the focus of current policy in the United States. To become more aligned with knowledge about youth development and learning, policy should: (1) shift away from a policy focus on content knowledge and standardized tests to a broader set of outcomes and measures, (2) proceed carefully with incorporating new measures into school accountability systems, and (3) provide the *"safe space"* for schools to become learning organizations.

The Current Policy Emphasis on Content Knowledge and Test-Based Accountability Undermines Practitioners' Ability to Provide Developmental Experiences

Policymakers have long been concerned about what preparation young people need for the future to become productive members of society. *"College and career readiness"* is the current mantra of the education policy

---

321   This report does not directly address how development of the key factors and foundational components may play out differently for different groups (e.g., by gender, sexual orientation, immigrant status, involvement in the juvenile

justice system) and what specific barriers, assets, and needs each subgroup may have. This is a critical area of investigation that should be pursued.

world, where making students *"college ready"* is often narrowly defined as building their content knowledge and academic skills. The broad adoption of the Common Core State Standards is a testament to how widespread this view is; 43 states and the District of Columbia have signed on to replace their previous state standards with the new Common Core to better prepare students for college. The prevailing narrative is one of *"gaps"* between what students know—particularly what low-income youth of color know—and what they need to know in the new economy. Within this narrative, preparing adolescents for young adulthood depends on broadening access to advanced coursework and implementing rigorous academic standards to ensure that all students graduate ready for college.

Because content knowledge and skills are seen as the pathway to a college degree and productive work, test scores that purport to measure such knowledge and skills have taken on an outsized importance in the educational landscape. Teachers are increasingly evaluated on their ability to produce high test scores, a metric that has become synonymous with *"effectiveness."* Even out-of-school programs are pressured to prove their worth by demonstrating impact on school achievement tests. Test scores have become the measure against which almost all educational interventions, pedagogical approaches, and curricular programs are currently judged. The emphasis on academic content knowledge, coupled with an expansion of accountability metrics based on standardized test scores, has led to a narrowing of the types of experiences practitioners are providing to young people. Arts, music, physical education, and other *"non-core"* subjects are eliminated to make instructional minutes for more math and reading, for example. Afterschool programs are asked to have a more academic focus to better prepare students for college and career. Teachers are reluctant to devote time to relationship-building in the classroom or otherwise addressing students' psycho-social needs because of the intense pressure to stay focused on content delivery.

Content knowledge is an essential part of what young people need to learn for the future, whether in school, at home, or in afterschool programs, but it is far from the only thing that matters. Policies that put too great an emphasis on content knowledge and standardized tests create incentives for practitioners to see the teaching of content knowledge as the sole outcome of interest. As this report has shown, the other foundational components not only facilitate engagement and learning of content knowledge, but they are also important developmental outcomes in and of themselves. Policies that promote these other foundational components would help to create conditions that foster both the learning of academic content and the development of young people more holistically.

Proceed Carefully with Incorporating *"Noncognitive"* Measures into Accountability Systems

The policy window for a more holistic approach to the development and learning of young people is opening; there is growing discontent over standardized testing. Recently, a movement to integrate alternative measures of student success into school accountability systems has gained some momentum, exemplified by the California *"CORE"* districts that have received No Child Left Behind waivers allowing them to include social-emotional factors and school climate measures in place of test scores as accountability metrics. This holistic approach to evaluating students is in alignment with the Foundations for Young Adult Success developmental framework; however, some caution is necessary when using these new measures for accountability purposes.

Many important questions remain about measuring noncognitive or social-emotional factors and about their suitability for an accountability system that was developed around standardized tests. When measuring a particular construct—for example, student self-efficacy—it is difficult to disentangle a student's prior level of self-efficacy from their gain or loss of self-efficacy as a result of being in a particular school or classroom or being taught by one teacher or another. Students make judgements about their self-efficacy based on their prior experiences and may have a different baseline sense of what their efficacy is. Further, self-efficacy seems to vary considerably from one task or content area to another. Likewise, there is much murkiness as to whether measured changes in noncognitive or social-emotional factors in a school context will be transferable to other contexts. Standards for the developmental trajectory on measures of noncognitive performance do not exist; also, it is not clear what constitutes a strong vs. weak

81

performance. The development of innovative and more traditional measures of noncognitive factors is a growing field, but further studies validating and better understanding the properties of these measures and how they are related to their intended use are needed before consolidating them into school accountability systems.

Policy Needs to Provide the *"Safe Space"* for Schools and Out-Of-School Programs to Become Learning Organizations

The ambitious vision given in the Foundations for Young Adult Success developmental framework does not provide a clear roadmap of specific practices, strategies, or programs to implement. Moving from the current approach to schooling to a more holistic and developmentally aligned approach will require trial and error. Just as young people need opportunities to tinker and practice in order to learn, practitioners also need opportunities for tinkering and practicing, as well as making mistakes, as they learn new ways of teaching and working with young people. In an age when accountability is a dominant way of managing schools, the space to make mistakes is very small. For real shifts to happen in educational practice, schools need to become learning organizations that provide opportunities for adults to learn, and policy needs to provide the *"safe space"* to do so.

For the Foundations for Young Adult Success developmental framework to become a guide for parents, caregivers, educators, and youth workers, we will need an equivalent effort to support these adults in building their capacity to create quality developmental experiences for youth, a strong identity as experts in supporting the growth of young people, and the agency to enact the framework in their daily work. To make this a reality, we need a policy focus on high-quality professional development that utilizes the developmental experiences outlined in the report. Parents and families can also benefit from having the opportunity to learn more about development and how children learn. Like the youth whom they serve, adults need opportunities to encounter, tinker, practice, choose, and contribute, and to make meaning through describing, evaluating, connecting, envisioning, and integrating. This means providing the resources and time needed to support deep professional communities and foster developmental relationships that promote good practice. It also means breaking down the siloes that exist between practitioners who work in the school and out-of-school settings so that learning can be shared.

Gaps in the Research

This report has drawn on the rich body of research evidence, theory, and practice wisdom and synthesized it into the Foundations for Young Adult Success developmental framework. Through this process we have identified knowledge gaps in what is needed to promote more effective policies and practices. One is in identifying specific developmental tasks that might have a *"critical window,"* after which it would be very difficult to achieve optimal development. Other gaps in knowledge surround the types of positive supports youth need for optimal development from early childhood through adolescence, or the *"dosage"* of particular kinds of experiences necessary to produce lasting and transferrable results.

What Practices and Strategies Promote the Development of Identity and Agency?

While researchers have learned a tremendous amount about development in the last several decades, many questions remain unanswered. In this report, we provided a developmental trajectory for the key factors for young adult success—competencies, agency, and an integrated identity. However, this relied on piecing together a number of existing theories; rarely if ever has the development of agency, for example, been studied longitudinally from early childhood through young adulthood. Theory has provided guidance on how an early sense of *"self"* underlies later identity formation, but this area is understudied in empirical research. While there is converging evidence that supports each of the developmental experiences we identify in this report, as well as the importance of developmental relationships, we do not know which specific combination of experiences would best promote the formation of integrated identity and agency. We also still lack a strong understanding of how all of the foundational components outlined here link directly to the development of competencies, integrated identity, and agency.

What Can Be Done to Intervene with Young People After Developmental Windows Close?

The Foundations for Young Adult Success developmental framework includes four foundational components—self-regulation, knowledge and skills, mindsets, and values—which are all crucial factors in a person's development toward optimal capacity. What happens if youth do not grow each of these foundational components in the developmental period during which they are most malleable? What types of interventions should we invest in—and for whom and at what period in their lives—if children seem to be falling behind? And for the youngest children, how can we even be sure that a child is falling outside of *"normative"* development, given how very wide the range of development is during the early years?

What Is the Interaction of Experiences in Different Settings?

This report also raises a number of questions about the experiences youth encounter in the various settings they inhabit on a daily basis. We know quite well that what youth experience in school often varies from their experiences with friends, at home, or even in other educational settings. What we do not know is the extent to which those experiences need to be coordinated and supportive of each other, even if they are not teaching the same skills. How much do practices at home support or inhibit what teachers, youth workers, and others aim to do with youth? How aligned do those practices need to be? And can effective practices in one setting ameliorate negative experiences in another setting?

How Can the Key Factors and Foundational Components Best Be Measured for Different Purposes?

Measurement is a core part of evaluating needs and gauging progress in any field. With the growing interest in factors other than academic content knowledge and skills, the number of assessments created to measure these factors has also grown. As discussed in the policy implications section, a number of questions about these factors and the assessments complicate their immedi-

ate implementation into practice. For example, it is very unclear whether a particular factor is best conceived as an individual characteristic that can be cultivated over time (analogous to a skill), or as a situational response to particular settings, opportunities, or expectations (similar to the concept of *"engagement,"* which can wax and wane from one moment to the next). Where it might make sense to measure growth over time in the first case, a different approach to measurement might be called for in the latter case. Further, it can be difficult to disentangle young people's prior capacities—what they walked into a setting with—from changes induced by the setting itself related to adult practice, opportunities for developmental relationships and developmental experiences, or the culture and climate of the place. In addition, neither are there standards for the developmental trajectory on these measures, nor are there thresholds for what young people need to have in order to attain a college degree, hold a family-sustaining job, or achieve any other markers of success in young adulthood.

Finally it will be important to clarify how these different assessments will be used and whether they are appropriate for the intended use.[322] Practitioners may want to be able to assess young people diagnostically prior to the beginning of the school year or program to determine how to best structure their practice in response to individual needs. They may also want assessments to measure progress in a formative way throughout their interactions with young people and adjust their practice as needed, in response to individual students and for the whole classroom or program. Finally, for both the student and classroom or program level, practitioners, administrators, and policymakers will want to have some means of making a summative judgment about performance and progress. Each of these uses will require a different type of assessment, and research has an important role to play in better understanding these assessments and shaping the discussion around their use.

In short, the demand for measures of noncognitive or social-emotional factors has far outpaced the state of the field of measurement for these same constructs.

---

322 See Duckworth & Yeager (2015) for a discussion of measures and their suitability for different purposes.

In a case such as this, there is great potential for measurement instruments to be misused, to produce faulty data, to conflate statistical significance with meaningfulness, or to otherwise lead practitioners down a fruitless path. We strongly urge caution in the use of measurement tools until the science of measuring these important constructs catches up with the interest in and demand for them.

Conclusion

We began this report by asking: What exactly do we hope our children will be able to accomplish as adults? What vision guides our work? How do we make that vision a reality for all children? The Foundations for Young Adult Success developmental framework is a first step in guiding practitioners, policymakers, parents, and researchers in working together around this vision, whether in reimagining how to coach a basketball team, reshaping policies in a local school district, selecting an afterschool program for one's child, or developing a study on measuring agency. Ensuring that young people grow into successful young adults requires investments in their learning and development from birth to young adulthood so that all of them have ongoing opportunities to truly reach their potential.

Making this vision a reality will require a collective responsibility for all young people. It means asking practitioners to question their own beliefs about what is possible and rethink how they work with young people on a day-to-day basis. It means asking policymakers to focus on a bigger picture and broader set of outcomes and to consider policies that would support the efforts of practitioners in developing young people. It means asking researchers to provide accessible, meaningful, and actionable answers to core questions of policy and practice. It means asking families to understand the needs of their children and work with the institutions they cross everyday so that these needs are met. It means asking for change both within existing institutions and structures while also asking what new institutions and structures might better serve our vision. Addressing the inequities of opportunities facing young adults will require more than equipping young people with the capacity to navigate the world as it exists now, it will mean that they are also able to envision and create a better world for future generations.

References

Achieve, Inc. (2012, November).
Transforming public reporting to ensure college and career readiness for ALL [Policy Brief]. Washington, DC: Achieve, Inc. and the American Diploma Project.

Agostin, T.M., & Bain, S.K. (1997).
Predicting early school success with developmental and social skills screeners. *Psychology in the Schools, 34*(3), 219-228.

Akers, J.F., Jones, R.M., & Coyl, D.D. (1998).
Adolescent friendship pairs: similarities in identity status development, behaviors, attitudes, and intentions. *Journal of Adolescent Research, 13*(2), 178–201.

Alasker, F., & Olweus, D. (1992).
Stability of global self-evaluations in early adolescence: A cohort longitudinal study. *Journal of Research in Adolescence, 2*(2), 123-145.

Arnett, J.J. (2000).
Emerging adulthood: A theory of development from the late teens through the twenties. *American Psychologist, 55*(5), 469-480.

Arnett, J.J. (2007).
Emerging adulthood: What is it, and what is it good for? *Child Development Perspectives, 1*(2), 68-73.

Ashforth, B.E., & Kreiner, G.E. (1999).
"How can you do it?": Dirty work and the challenge of constructing a positive identity. *Academy of Management Review, 24*(3), 413-434.

Astin, A.W. (1993).
What matters in college? Four critical years revisited. San Francisco, CA: Jossey-Bass.

Atkinson, J.W. (1957).
Motivational determinants or risk-taking behavior. *Psychological Review, 64*(6), 359-372.

Aud, S., Hussar, W., Johnson, F., Kena, G., Roth, E., Manning, E., Wang, X., & Zhang, J. (2012).
The condition of education 2012 (NCES 2012-045). Washington, DC: U.S. Department of Education, National Center for Education Statistics. Retrieved from https://nces.ed.gov/pubsearch/pubsinfo.asp?pubid=2012045

Bandura, A. (1986).
Social foundations of thought and action: A social cognitive theory. Englewood Cliffs, NJ: Prentice-Hall.

Bandura, A. (1993).
Perceived self-efficacy in cognitive development and functioning. *Educational Psychologist, 28*(2), 117-148.

Bandura, A. (2006).
Toward a psychology of human agency. *Perspectives on Psychological Science, 1*(2), 164-180.

Bandura, A., & Schunk, D.H. (1981).
Cultivating competence, self-efficacy, and intrinsic interest through proximal self-motivation. *Journal of Personality and Social Psychology, 41*(3), 586-598.

Bannister, D., & Agnew, J. (1976).
The child's construing of self. *Nebraska Symposium on Motivation, 24*, 99-125.

Barrick, M.R., & Mount, M.K. (1991).
The big five personality dimensions and job performance: A meta-analysis. *Personal Psychology, 44*(1), 1-26.

Baumeister, R.F., Vohs, K.D., Aaker, J.L., & Garbinsky, E.N. (2013).
Some key differences between a happy life and a meaningful life. *Journal of Positive Psychology, 8*(6), 505-516.

Benson, P.L. (2008).
Sparks: How parents can help ignite the hidden strengths of teenagers. San Francisco, CA: Jossey-Bass.

Benson, P.L., & Scales, P.C. (2009).
The definition and preliminary measurement of thriving in adolescence. *Journal of Positive Psychology, 4*(1), 85-104.

Berger, P.L., & Luckmann, T. (1966).
The Social Construction of Reality. Garden City, NY: Anchor.

Berger, R. (2003).
An ethic of excellence: Building a culture of craftsmanship with students. Portsmouth, NH: Heinemann.

Berk, L.E. (2007).
Development through the lifespan (4th ed.). Boston, MA: Allyn and Bacon.

Berk, L.E., Mann, T.D., & Ogan, A.T. (2006).
Make-believe play: Wellspring for development of self-regulation. In D.G. Singer, R.M. Golinkoff, & K. Hirsh-Pasek (Eds.), *Play=learning: How play motivates and enhances children's cognitive and social-emotional growth* (pp.74-100). New York, NY: Oxford University Press.

Berliner, D.C. (2009).
Poverty and potential: Out-of-school factors and school success. Boulder, CO and Tempe, AZ: Education and the Public Interest Center, University of Colorado/Education Policy Research Unit, Arizona State University. Retrieved from http://epicpolicy.org/publication/poverty-and-potential

Berzonsky, M.D. (1989).
Identity style: Conceptualization and measurement. *Journal of Adolescent Research, 4*(3), 268-282.

Blair, C. (2002).
School readiness: Integrating cognition and emotion in a neurobiological conceptualization of children's functioning at school entry. *American Psychologist, 57*(2), 111-127.

Blair, C., & Razza, R.P. (2007).
Relating effortful control, executive function, and false belief understanding to emerging math and literacy ability in kindergarten. *Child Development, 78*(2), 647-663.

Blakemore, S.J., & Choudhury, S. (2006).
Development of the adolescent brain: implications for executive function and social cognition. *Journal of Child Psychology and Psychiatry, 47*(3-4), 296-312.

Bodrova, E., Germeroth, C., & Leong, D.J. (2013).
Play and self-regulation: Lessons from Vygotsky. *American Journal of Play, 6*(1), 111-123.

Bouffard-Bouchard, T. (1990).
Influence of self-efficacy on performance in a cognitive task. *The Journal of Social Psychology, 130*(3), 353-363.

Bowlby, J. (1982).
Attachment and loss: Retrospect and prospect. *American Journal of Orthopsychiatry, 52*(4), 664-678.

Bowles, S., & Gintis, H. (1976).
Schooling in capitalist America. New York, NY: Basic Books.

Bowles, S., & Gintis, H. (2002).
Schooling in capitalist America revisited. *Sociology of Education, 75*(1), 1-18.

Braithwaite, V.A., & Law, H.G. (1985).
Structure of human values: Testing the adequacy of the Rokeach Value Survey. *Journal of Personality and Social Psychology, 49*(1), 250.

Bransford, J.D., Brown, A.L., & Cocking, R.R. (Eds.). (2000).
How people learn: Brain, mind, experience, and school (Expanded edition). Washington, DC: National Academies Press.

Bredekamp, S. (1987).
Developmentally appropriate practice in early childhood programs serving children from birth through age 8. Washington, DC: National Association for the Education of Young Children.

Bronfenbrenner, U. (1977).
Toward an experimental ecology of human development. *American Psychologist, 32*(7), 513-531.

Bronfenbrenner, U. (1979).
The ecology of human development: Experiments by nature and design. Cambridge, MA: Harvard University Press.

Bronfenbrenner, U. (1986).
Ecology of the family as a context for human development: Research perspectives. *Developmental Psychology, 22*(6), 723.

Bronson, M. (2000).
Self-regulation in early childhood: Nature and nurture. New York, NY: Guilford Press.

Brown, A.L., & DeLoache, J.S. (1978).
Skills, plans, and self-regulation. In R. Siegler (Ed.), *Children's thinking: What develops?* (pp. 3-35). Hillsdale, NJ: Erlbaum.

Brown, B.B. (1990).
Peer groups and peer cultures. In S.S. Feldman & G.R. Elliott (Eds.), *At the threshold: The developing adolescent* (pp.171-196). Cambridge, MA: Harvard University Press.

Bureau of Labor Statistics. (2013, April 17).
Economic news release: College enrollment and work activity of 2012 high school graduates (USDL-13-0670). Washington, DC. Retrieved from www.bls.gov/news.release/hsgec.nr0.htm

Campbell, F.A., & Ramey, C.T. (1995).
Cognitive and school outcomes for high-risk African-American students at middle adolescence: Positive effects of early intervention. *American Educational Research Journal, 32*(4), 743-772.

Casey, B.J., Getz, S., & Galvan, A. (2008).
The adolescent brain. *Developmental Review, 28*(1), 62-77.

Casner-Lott, J., & Barrington, L. (2006).
Are they really ready to work? Employers' perspectives on the basic knowledge and applied skills of new entrants to the 21st century U.S. workforce. Washington, DC: The Conference Board, Corporate Voices for Working Families, Partnership for 21st Century Skills, & Society for Human Resource Management.

Caspi, A., Henry, B., McGee, R.O., Moffitt, T.E., & Silva, P.A. (1995).
Temperamental origins of child and adolescent behavior problems: From age three to age fifteen. *Child Development, 66*(1), 55-68.

Center on the Developing Child at Harvard University. (2004).
Young children develop in an environment of relationships (Working Paper No. 1). Cambridge, MA: Harvard University. Retrieved from http://developingchild.harvard.edu/resources/reports_and_working_papers/working_papers/wp1/

Center on the Developing Child at Harvard University. (2011).
Building the brain's "Air Traffic Control" system: How early experiences shape the development of executive function (Working Paper No. 11). Cambridge, MA: Harvard University. Retrieved from http://developing-child.harvard.edu/index.php/resources/reports_and_working_papers/working_papers/wp11/

Center on the Developing Child at Harvard University. (2012).
The science of neglect: The persistent absence of responsive care disrupts the developing brain (Working Paper No. 12). Cambridge, MA: Harvard University. Retrieved from http://developingchild.harvard.edu/index.php/resources/reports_and_working_papers/working_papers/wp12/

Certo, J.L., Cauley, K.M., & Chafin, C. (2003).
Students' perspectives on their high school experience.
Adolescence, 38(152), 705-724.

Chavez, A.F., & Guido-DiBrito, F. (1999).
Racial and ethnic identity and development.
*New Directions for Adult and Continuing Education,
1999*(84), 39-47.

Cheng, C., Sanchez-Burks, J., & Lee, F. (2008).
Connecting the dots within: Creative performance
and identity integration. *Psychological Science, 19*(11),
1178-1184.

Chess, S., & Thomas, A. (1977).
Temperamental individuality from childhood to
adolescence. *Journal of the American Academy of
Child Psychiatry, 16*(2), 218-226.

Chetty, R., Hendren, N., Kline, P., Saez, E., & Turner, N. (2014a).
Is the United States still a land of opportunity? Recent
trends in intergenerational mobility. *American Economic
Review, American Economic Association, 104*(5), 141-147.

Chetty, R., Hendren, N., Kline, P., & Saez, E., (2014b).
*Where is the land of opportunity? The geography of
intergenerational mobility in the United States. (NBER
Working Paper 19843)*. Washington, DC: National Bureau
of Economic Research. Retrieved from http://www.nber.
org/papers/w19843

Clotfelter, C.T., Ladd, H.F., & Vigdor, J.L. (2009).
The academic achievement gap in grades 3 to 8. *The
Review of Economics and Statistics, 91*(2), 398-419.

Cole, P.M., Armstrong, L.M., & Pemberton, C.K. (2010).
The role of language in the development of emotion
regulation. In S.D.C.M.A. Bell (Ed.), *Child development
at the intersection of emotion and cognition* (pp. 59-77).
Washington, DC: American Psychological Association.

The Collaborative for Building After-School Systems (2013).
CBASS Measurement System. New York, NY: Author.

Collins, W.A., & Steinberg, L. (2006).
Adolescent development in interpersonal context.
In W. Damon, N. Eisenberg, & R.M. Lerner (Eds.),
Handbook of Child Psychology (Vol. 4) (pp. 1003-1067).
New York, NY: John Wiley & Sons, Inc.

The Committee for Children. (2011).
Early learning review of research. Seattle, WA: Author.
Retrieved from http://www.cfchildren.org/Portals/0/
SS_EL/EL_DOC/EL_Review_Research_SS.pdf

Conley, D. (2012).
A complete definition of college and career readiness.
Eugene, OR: Educational Policy Improvement Center
Publications. Retrieved from https://www.epiconline.org/
publications/documents/College%20and%20Career%20
Readiness%20Definition.pdf

Conley, D.T. (2014).
*Getting ready for college, careers, and the Common Core:
What every educator needs to know.* San Francisco, CA:
Jossey-Bass/Wiley.

Copple, C., & Bredekamp, S. (2009).
*Developmentally appropriate practice in early childhood
programs serving children from birth through age 8.*
Washington, DC: National Association for the Education
of Young Children.

Côté, J.E. (1996).
Identity: A multidimensional analysis. In G.R. Adams,
R., Montemayor, & T.P. Gullotta (Eds.), *Psychosocial
development during adolescence: Progress in developmental
contextualism* (pp. 130-180). Thousand Oaks, CA: Sage.

Côté, J.E. (2009).
Identity formation and self-development in adolescence.
In R.M. Lerner & L. Steinberg (Eds.), *Handbook of adoles-
cent psychology, 3rd ed.* (Vol. 1) (pp. 266-304). New York,
NY: John Wiley & Sons, Inc.

Covington, M.V. (1984).
The self-worth theory of achievement motivation: Findings
and implications. *The Elementary School Journal, 85*(1), 4-20.

Currie, J., & Thomas, D. (1999).
*Early test scores, socioeconomic status and future outcomes
(No. w6943).* Cambridge, MA: National Bureau of Economic
Research.

Curtis, A. (1998).
A curriculum for the pre-school child (2nd ed.). New York,
NY: Routledge.

Cury, F., Elliot, A.J., Fonseca, D.D., & Moller, A.C. (2006).
The social-cognitive model of achievement motivation
and the 2×2 achievement goal framework. *Journal of
Personality and Social Psychology, 90*(4), 666-679.

Damon, W. (2008).
*The path to purpose: Helping our children find their calling
in life.* New York, NY: The Free Press.

Davis, E.P., Glynn, L.M., Schetter, C.D., Hobel, C.,
Chicz-Demet, A., Sandman, C.A. (2007).
Prenatal exposure to maternal depression and cortisol
influences infant temperament. *Journal of the American
Academy of Child and Adolescent Psychiatry, 46*(6), 737-746.

Deci, E.L., & Ryan, R.M. (1985).
*Intrinsic motivation and self-determination in human
behavior.* New York, NY: Plenum Press.

DeLoache, J.S., Miller, K.F., & Pierroutsakos, S.L. (1998).
Reasoning and problem-solving. In D. Kuhn & R.S. Siegler
(Eds.), *Handbook of Child Psychology* (Vol. 2) (pp. 801-850).
New York, NY: John Wiley & Sons, Inc.

Delpit, L. (1988).
The silenced dialogue: Power and pedagogy in educating
other people's children. *Harvard Educational Review, 58*(3),
280-299.

Delpit, L. (1995).
Teachers, culture, and power: An interview with Lisa Delpit. In D. Levine, R. Lowe, B. Peterson, & R. Tenorio (Eds.), *Rethinking schools: An agenda for change* (pp. 136–147). New York, NY: The New Press.

Deutsch, N.L. (2008).
Pride in the projects: Teens building identities in urban contexts. New York, NY: New York University Press.

Dewey, J. (1938/1969).
Experience and education. New York, NY: Collier.

DeWit, D., Karioja, K., & Rye, B. (2010).
Student perceptions of diminished teacher and classmate support following the transition to high school. Are they related to declining attendance? *School Effectiveness and School Improvement, 21*(4), 451-472.

Diamond, A. (2000).
Close interrelation of motor development and cognitive development and of the cerebellum and prefrontal cortex. *Child Development, 71*(1), 44-56.

Diamond, A., & Lee, K. (2011).
Interventions shown to aid executive function development in children 4 to 12 years old. *Science, 333*(6045), 959-964.

Dignam, J.M. (1990).
Personality structure: Emergence of the five-factor model. *Annual Review of Psychology, 41*(1), 417-440.

DuBois, D.L., Bull, C.A., Sherman, M.D., & Roberts, M. (1998).
Self-esteem and adjustment in early adolescence: A social-contextual perspective. *Journal of Youth and Adolescence, 27*(5), 557-583.

Duckworth, A.L., & Yeager, D.S. (2015).
Measurement matters assessing personal qualities other than cognitive ability for educational purposes. *Educational Researcher, 44*(4), 237-251.

Duncan, G.J., & Magnuson, K. (2011).
The nature and impact of early achievement skills, attention skills, and behavior problems. In G.J. Duncan & R.J. Murnane (Eds.), *Whither Opportunity? Rising inequality, schools, and children's life chances* (pp. 47-69). New York, NY: Russell Sage Foundation.

Duncan, G.J., & Murnane, R.J. (Eds.). (2011).
Whither opportunity? Rising inequality, schools, and children's life chances. New York, NY: Russell Sage Foundation.

Dutton, J.E., Roberts, L.M., & Bedhar, J. (2010).
Pathways for positive identity construction at work. Four types of positive identity and the building of social resources. *Academy of Management Review, 35*(2), 265-293.

Dweck, C.S. (1975).
The role of expectations and attributions in the alleviation of learned helplessness. *Journal of Personality and Social Psychology, 31*(4), 674-685.

Dweck, C.S. (2002).
Messages that motivate: How praise molds students' beliefs, motivation, and performance (in surprising ways). In J. Aronson (Ed.), *Improving academic achievement: Impact of psychological factors on education* (pp. 37-60). San Diego, CA: Academic Press.

Dweck, C.S. (2006).
Mindset: The new psychology of success. New York, NY: Random House.

Dweck, C.S., & Leggett, E.L. (1988).
A social-cognitive approach to motivation and personality. *Psychological Review, 95*(2), 256-273.

Eccles, J.S. (1999).
The development of children ages 6 to 14. *Future of Children, 9*(2), 30-44.

Eccles, J.S. (2009).
Who am I and what am I going to do with my life? Personal and collective identities as motivators of action. *Educational Psychologist, 44*(2), 78-89.

Eccles J.S., Adler, T.F., Futterman, R., Goff, S.B., Kaczala, C.M., Meece, J.L., & Midgley, C. (1983).
Expectancies, values, and academic behaviors. In J.T. Spence (Ed.), *Achievement and achievement motivation* (pp. 75-146). San Francisco, CA: W. H. Freeman.

Eccles, J.S., Lord, S., & Midgley, C. (1991).
What are we doing to early adolescents? The impact of educational contexts on early adolescents. *American Journal of Education, 99*(4), 521-542.

Eccles, J.S., & Midgley, C. (1989).
Stage/environment fit: Developmentally appropriate classrooms for early adolescents. In R.E. Ames & C. Ames (Eds.), *Research on motivation in education* (Vol. 3) (pp. 139-186). San Diego, CA: Academic Press.

Eccles, J.S., Midgley, C., & Adler, T.F. (1984).
Grade-related changes in the school environment: Effects on achievement motivation. In J.G. Nicholls (Ed.), *The development of achievement motivation* (pp. 283-331). Greenwich, CT: JAI Press.

Eccles, J.S., Midgley, C., Wigfield, A., Buchanan, C.M., Reuman, D., Flanagan, C., & Mac Iver, D. (1993).
Development during adolescence: The impact of stage-environment fit on young adolescents' experiences in schools and in families. *American Psychologist, 48*(2), 90.

Education Trust. (2012).
Advancing to completion: Increasing degree attainment by improving graduation rates and closing gaps for African-American students. Washington, DC: The Education Trust. Retrieved from http://www.edtrust.org/dc/publication/advancing-to-completion-increasing-degree-attainment-by-improving-graduation-rates-a-0

Eisenberg, N., & Fabes, R.A. (1992).
Emotion, regulation, and the development of social competence. In M.S. Clark (Ed.), *Emotion and social behavior. Review of personality and social psychology* (pp. 119-150). Thousand Oaks, CA: Sage Publications.

Elias, M.J., & Zins, J.E. (2012).
Bullying, peer harassment, and victimization in the schools: The next generation of prevention. New York, NY: Routledge.

Emirbayer, M., & Mische, A. (1998).
What is agency? *American Journal of Sociology, 103*(4), 962-1023.

Ericsson, K.A., & Charness, N. (1994).
Expert performance: Its structure and acquisition. *American Psychological Association, 49*(8), 725-747.

Ericsson, K.A., Krampe, R.T., & Tesch-Römer, C. (1993).
The role of deliberate practice in the acquisition of expert performance. *Psychological Review, 100*(3), 363-406.

Erikson, E. (1950/1963).
Childhood and Society (2nd ed.). New York, NY: W.W. Norton & Co.

Erikson, E.H. (1968).
Identity, youth and crisis. New York, NY: W.W. Norton & Co.

Espinoza-Herold, M. (2003).
Issues in Latino education: Race, school culture, and the politics of academic success. Boston, MA: Pearson Education Group.

Evans, G.W., & Schamberg, M.A. (2009).
Childhood poverty, chronic stress, and adult working memory. *Proceedings of the National Academy of Sciences, 106*(16), 6545-6549.

Expeditionary Learning (2014).
Revitalize Rochester. Retrieved from http://centerforstudentwork.elschools.org/projects/revitalize-rochester

Farrington, C.A., Roderick, M., Allensworth, E., Nagaoka, J., Keyes, T.S., Johnson, D.W., & Beechum, N.O. (2012).
Teaching adolescents to become learners: The role of noncognitive factors in shaping school performance. Chicago, IL: University of Chicago Consortium on Chicago School Research.

Feiler, D.C., Tost, L.P., & Grant, A.M. (2012).
Mixed reasons, missed giving: The costs of blending egoistic and altruistic reasons in donation requests. *Journal of Experimental Psychology, 48*(6), 1322-1328.

Fishbach, A., & Trope, Y. (2005).
The substitutability of external control and self-control in overcoming temptation. *Journal of Experimental Social Psychology, 41*(3), 256-270.

Fishbach, A., Zhang, Y., & Trope, Y. (2010).
Counteractive evaluation: Asymmetic shifts in the implicit value of conflicting motivations. *Journal of Experimental Social Psychology, 46*(1), 29-38.

Fitzsimons, G.M., & Finkel, E.J. (2011).
Outsourcing self-regulation. *Psychological Science, 22*(3), 369-375.

Flavell, J.H. (1977).
Cognitive development. Englewood Cliffs, NJ: Prentice-Hall.

Flavell, J.H. (1979).
Metacognition and cognitive monitoring: A new area of cognitive–developmental inquiry. *American Psychologist, 34*(10), 906-911.

Foulks, B., & Morrow, R.D. (1989).
Academic survival skills for the young child at risk for school failure. *The Journal of Educational Research, 82*(3), 158-165.

Fox, N.A., Almas, A.N., Degnan, K.A., Nelson, C.A., & Zeanah, C.H. (2011).
The effects of severe psychosocial deprivation and foster care intervention on cognitive development at 8 years of age: findings from the Bucharest Early Intervention Project. *Journal of Child Psychology and Psychiatry, 52*(9), 919-928.

Fredricks, J.A., Blumenfeld, P.C., & Paris, A.H. (2004).
School engagement: Potential of the concept, state of the evidence. *Review of educational research, 74*(1), 59-109.

Freire, P. (1970/1993).
Pedagogy of the oppressed. London, UK: Penguin Books.

Fryer, R.G., & Levitt, S.D. (2006).
The black-white test score gap through third grade. *American Law and Economics Review, 8*(2), 249-281.

Gecas, V. (2003).
Self-agency and the life course. In J.T. Mortimer & M.J. Shanahan (Eds.), *Handbook of the Life Course* (pp. 369-388). New York, NY: Springer Science+Business Media, LLC.

Gestsdottir, S., & Lerner, R.M. (2008).
Positive development in adolescence: The development and role of intentional self-regulation. *Human Development, 51*(3), 202.

Goldin, C.D., & Katz, L.F. (2008).
Transitions: Career and family life cycles of the educational elite. *The American Economic Review, 98*(2), 363-369.

Goldin, C.D., & Katz, L.F. (2009).
The race between education and technology. Cambridge, MA: Harvard University Press.

Goldsmith, H.H., Buss, A.H., Plomin, R., Rothbart, M.K., Thomas, A., Chess, S., . . . McCall, R.B. (1987).
Roundtable: What is temperament? Four approaches. *Child Development, 58*(2), 505-529.

González, N., Moll, L., & Amanti, C. (Eds.). (2005).
Funds of knowledge: Theorizing practices in households, communities, and classrooms. Mahwah, NJ: Lawrence Erlbaum Associates.

89

Gopnik, A. (2009).
The philosophical baby: What children's minds tell us about truth, love, and the meaning of life. New York, NY: Harper Collins Publisher.

Gorman-Smith, D., Henry, D.B., & Tolan, P.H. (2004).
Exposure to community violence and violence perpetration: The protective effects of family functioning. *Journal of Clinical Child and Adolescent Psychology, 33*(3), 439-449.

Gottfredson, M.R., & Hirschi, T. (1990).
A general theory of crime. Stanford, CA: Stanford University Press.

Gould, T. (Ed.). (2011).
Guardian of democracy: The civic mission of schools. Philadelphia, PA: The Leonore Annenberg Institute for Civics of the Annenberg Public Policy Center at the University of Pennsylvania and the Campaign for the Civic Mission of Schools.

Grant, A.M. (2008).
Does intrinsic motivation fuel the prosocial fire? Motivational synergy in predicting persistence, performance, and productivity. *Journal of Applied Psychology, 93*(1), 48-58.

Grant, A.M., & Hofmann, D.A. (2011).
It's not all about me motivating hand hygiene among health care professionals by focusing on patients. *Psychological Science, 22*(12), 1494-1499.

Guardo, C.J., & Bohan, J.B. (1971).
Development of a sense of self-identity in children. *Child Development, 42*(6), 1909-1921.

Gutgesell, M.E., & Payne, N. (2004).
Issues of adolescent psychological development in the 21st century. *Pediatrics in Review, 25*(3), 79-85.

Hacker, D.J., Dunlosky, J., & Graesser, A.C. (2009).
Handbook of metacognition in education. New York, NY: Routledge.

Halpern, R., Heckman, P.E., & Larson, R.W. (2013).
Realizing the potential of learning in middle adolescence. West Hills, CA: The Sally and Dick Roberts Coyote Foundation.

Hamilton, C.E. (2000).
Continuity and discontinuity of attachment from infancy through adolescence. *Child Development, 71*(3), 690-694.

Hart, B., & Risley, T. (1995).
Meaningful differences in the everyday experience of young American children. Baltimore, MD: Paul H. Brookes.

Harter, S. (1982).
The perceived competence scale for children. *Child Development, 53*(1), 87-97.

Harter, S. (1998).
The development of self-representations. In W. Damon & N. Eisenberg (Eds.), *Handbook of child psychology, 5th ed. Social, emotional, and personality development* (Vol. 3) (pp. 553-617). New York, NY: John Wiley & Sons, Inc.

Harter, S., & Monsour, A. (1992).
Developmental analysis of conflict caused by opposing attributes in the adolescent self-portrait. *Developmental Psychology, 28*(2), 251-260.

Harter, S., Waters, P., & Whitesell, N.R. (1998).
Relational self-worth: Differences in perceived worth as a person across interpersonal contexts among adolescents. *Child Development, 69*(3), 756-766.

Harvey, O.J., & Schroder, H.M. (1963).
Cognitive aspects of self and motivation. In O. Harvey (Ed.), *Motivation and social interaction: Cognitive determinants* (pp. 95-133). New York, NY: The Ronald Press Co.

Hattie, J., & Yates, G. (2014).
Visible learning and the science of how we learn. New York, NY: Routledge.

Hazen, E., Schlozman, S., & Beresin, E. (2008).
Adolescent psychological development: A review. *Pediatrics in Review, 29*(5), 161-168.

Heckman, J.J. (2008).
The Case for Investing in Disadvantaged Young Children. In *Big Ideas for Children: Investing in Our Nation's Future* (pp. 49-58). Washington, DC: First Focus.

Heckman, J.J., Pinto, R., & Savelyev, P.A. (2013).
Understanding the mechanisms through which an influential early childhood program boosted adult outcomes. *American Economic Review, 103*(6), 2052-2086.

Hernandez, M., & Iyengar, S.S. (2001).
What drives whom? A cultural perspective on human agency. *Columbia University Business School of Social Cognition, 19*(3), 269-294.

Heron, T. (2008).
Globalization, neoliberalism and the exercise of human agency. *International Journal of Politics, Culture, and Society, 20*(1-4), 85-101.

Hewlett Foundation. (2013).
Deeper learning competencies. Retrieved from http://www.hewlett.org/uploads/documents/Deeper_Learning_Defined__April_2013.pdf

Hidi, S., & Renninger, K.A. (2006).
The four-phase model of interest development. *Educational Psychologist, 41*(2), 111-127.

Hoff, E. (2003).
The specificity of environmental influence: Socioeconomic status affects early vocabulary development via maternal speech. *Child Development, 74*(5), 1368-1378.

Hogue, A., & Steinberg, L. (1995).
Homophily of internalized distress in adolescent peer groups. *Developmental Psychologist, 31*(6), 897-906.

Howse, R.B., Calkins, S.D., Anastopoulos, A.D., Keane, S.P., Shelton, T.L. (2003).
Regulatory contributors to children's kindergarten achievement. *Early Education and Development, 14*(1), 101-120.

90

Hughes, E.C. (1958).
Men and their work. Glencoe, IL: Free Press.

Hughes, E.C. (1962).
Good people and dirty work. *Social Problems, 10*(1), 3-11.

Huizink, A.C., Robles de Medina, P.G., Mulder, E.J.,
Visser, G.H., Buitelaar, J.K. (2003).
Stress during pregnancy is associated with developmental outcome in infancy. *Journal of Child Psychology and Psychiatry, 44*(6), 810-818.

Hulleman, C.S., & Harackiewicz, J.M. (2009).
Making education relevant: Increasing interest and performance in high school science classes. *Science, 326,* 1410-1412.

Huttenlocher, J., Vasilyeva, M., Waterfall, H., Vevea, J., Hedges, L.V. (2007).
The varieties of speech to young children. *Developmental Psychology, 43*(5), 1062-1083.

Huttenlocher, J., Waterfall, H., Vasilyeva, M., Vevea, J., & Hedges, L.V. (2010).
Sources of variability in children's language growth. *Cognitive Psychology, 61*(4), 343-365.

International Youth Foundation. (2013).
Getting youth in the door: Defining soft skills requirements for entry-level service sector jobs. Baltimore, MD: Author.

Irby, M., Pittman, K.J., & Tolman, J. (2003).
Blurring the lines: Expanding learning opportunities for children and youth. *New Directions for Youth Development, 2003*(97), 13-27.

Ito, M., Gutiérrez, K., Livingstone, S.,...Craig, S. (2013).
Connected learning: An agenda for research and design. Irvine, CA: Digital Media and Learning Research Hub.

James, W. (1912).
Essays in radical empiricism. New York, NY: Longmans, Green.

Jones, J.C. (1992).
Design method, Vol. 4. New York, NY: John Wiley & Sons, Inc.

Jones, S.M., & Bailey, R. (2014, January).
An organizing model for social-emotional learning. Presented at the National Governors' Association Cross-State Policy Academy Meeting II, Washington, DC.

Kaushal, N., Magnuson, K., & Waldfogel, J. (2011).
How is family income related to investments in children's learning? In G.J. Duncan & R.J. Murnane (Eds.), *Whither Opportunity? Rising inequality, schools, and children's life chances* (pp. 187-206). New York: Russell Sage Foundation.

Keeton, M.T., Sheckley, B.G., & Griggs, J.K. (2002).
Efficiency and effectiveness in higher education. Dubuque, IA: Kendall/Hunt Publishing Company.

Kids First Oakland (2008).
Affordable youth transportation to school. Retrieved from http://www.kidsfirstoakland.org/index.php?s=96

Kolb, A.Y., & Kolb, D.A. (2009).
The learning way: Meta-cognition aspects of experiential learning. *Simulation Gaming, 40*(3), 297-327.

Kolb, D. (1984).
Experiential learning: Experience as a source of learning and development. Upper Saddle River, NJ: Prentice Hall.

Kroger, J. (1993).
Ego identity: An overview. In J. Kroger (Ed.), *Discussions on ego identity* (pp. 1-20). Hillsdale, NJ: Erlbaum.

Kupersmidt, J.B., & Coie, J.D. (1990).
Preadolescent peer status, aggression, and school adjustment as predictors of externalizing problems in adolescence. *Child Development, 61*(5), 1350-1362.

Labov, W. (1982).
Competing value systems in the inner city schools. In P. Gilmore & A. Glathorn (Eds.), *Children in and out of school: Ethnography and education* (pp. 148-171). Washington, DC: Center for Applied Linguistics.

Ladd, G.W., & Price, J.M. (1986).
Promoting children's cognitive and social competence: The relation between parents' perceptions of task difficulty and children's perceived and actual competence. *Child Development, 57*(2), 446-460.

Lally, P., Van Jaarsveld, C.H.M., Potts, H.W.W., & Wardle, J. (2010).
How are habits formed: Modelling habit formation in the real world. *European Journal of Social Psychology, 40*(6), 998-1009.

Lareau, A. (2003).
Unequal childhoods: Class, race, and family life. Berkeley, CA: University of California Press.

Lave, J., & Wenger, E. (1991).
Situated learning: Legitimate peripheral participation. Cambridge, MA: Cambridge University Press.

Leffel, K., & Suskind, D. (2013, November).
Parent-directed approaches to enrich the early language environments of children living in poverty. *Seminars in Speech and Language, 42*(4), 267-278.

Lennon, J.M. (2010).
Self-efficacy. In J.A. Rosen, E.J. Glennie, B.W. Dalton, J.M. Lennon, & R.N. Bozick (Eds.), *Noncognitive skills in the classroom: New perspectives on educational research* (pp. 91-115). Research Triangle Park, NC: RTI Press/RTI International.

Lerner, R.M., Brentano, C., Dowling, E.M., & Anderson, P.M. (2002).
Positive youth development: Thriving as the basis of personhood and civil society. *New Directions for Youth Development, 2002*(95), 11-33.

Li, J., & Julian, M. (2012).
Developing relationships as the active ingredient: A unifying working hypothesis of "what works" across intervention settings. *American Journal of Orthopsychiatry, 82*(2), 157-166.

Lippman, L., Atienza, A., Rivers, A., & Keith, J. (2008).
A developmental perspective on college & workplace readiness. Washington, DC: Child Trends.

Liu, J. (2004).
Childhood externalizing behavior: theory and implications. *Journal of Child and Adolescent Psychiatric Nursing, 17*(3), 93-103.

Livesley, W.J., & Bromley, D.B. (1973).
Person perception in childhood and adolescence. Oxford, England: John Wiley & Sons, Inc.

Locke, E.A., & Latham, G.P. (2002).
Building a practically useful theory of goal setting and task motivation: A 35-year odyssey. *American Psychologist, 57*(9), 705.

Loewenstein, G. (1996).
Out of control: Visceral influences on behavior. *Organizational Behavior and Human Decision Processes, 65*(5003), 272-292.

Loman, M.M., & Gunnar, M.R. (2010).
Early experience and the development of stress reactivity and regulation in children. *Neuroscience and Biobehavioral Reviews, 34*(6), 867-876.

Luria, A.R. (1961).
The role of speech in the regulation of normal and abnormal behavior. New York, NY: Liveright.

Luster, T., & McAdoo, H.P. (1995).
Factors related to self-esteem among African American youths: A secondary analysis of the High/Scope Perry Preschool data. *Journal of Research on Adolescence, 5*(4), 451-467.

Mahoney, J.L., Lord, H., & Carryl, E. (2005).
An ecological analysis of after-school program participation and the development of academic performance and motivational attributes for disadvantaged children. *Child Development, 76*(4), 811-825.

Marcia, J. (1966).
Development and validation of ego-identity status. *Journal of Personality and Social Psychology, 3*(5), 551–558.

Marks, H. (2000).
Student engagement in instructional activity: Patterns in the elementary, middle, and high school years. *American Educational Research Journal, 37*(1), 153-184.

Markus, H.R., & Kitayama, S. (1991).
Culture and the self: Implications for cognition, emotion, and motivation. *Psychological Review, 98*(2), 224-253.

Markus, H., & Kunda, Z. (1986).
Stability and malleability of the self-concept. *Journal of Personality and Social Psychology, 51*(4), 858-866.

Markus, H.J., & Nurius, P.S. (1984).
Self-understanding and self-regulation in middle childhood. In National Research Council (Ed.), *Development during middle childhood: The years from six to twelve* (pp. 147-183). Washington, DC: National Academies.

Massey, D., & Denton, N. (1993).
American Apartheid: Segregation and the Making of the Underclass. Cambridge, MA: Harvard University Press.

Mayseless, O., & Keren, E. (2014).
Finding a meaningful life as a developmental task in emerging adulthood: The domains of love and work across cultures. *Emerging Adulthood, 2*(1), 63-73.

McAdams, D.P., & Adler, J.M. (2010).
Autobiographical memory and the construction of a narrative identity: Theory, research, and clinical implications. In J.E. Maddux & J. Tangney (Eds.), *Social psychological foundations of clinical psychology* (pp. 36-50). New York, NY: Guilford Press.

McClelland, M.M., Acock, A.C., & Morrison, F.J. (2006).
The impact of kindergarten learning-related skills on academic trajectories at the end of elementary school. *Early Childhood Research Quarterly, 21*(4), 471-490.

McClelland, M.M., Cameron, C.E., Connor, C.M., Farris, C.L., Jewkes, A.M., & Morrison, F.J. (2007).
Links between behavioral regulation and preschoolers' literacy, vocabulary, and math skills. *Developmental Psychology, 43*(4), 947.

McClelland, M.M., Morrison, F.J., & Holmes, D.L. (2000).
Children at risk for early academic problems: The role of learning-related social skills. *Early Childhood Research Quarterly, 15*(3), 307-329.

McCrae, R.R. (1996).
Social consequences of experiential openness. *Psychological Bulletin, 120*(3), 323.

McCrae, R.R., & Costa, P.T. (1997).
Conceptions and correlates of openness to experience. In R. Hogan, J. Johnson, & S.R. Briggs (Eds.), *Handbook of personality psychology* (pp. 825-847). San Diego, CA: Academic Press.

McCrae, R.R., Costa Jr., P.T., Terracciano, A., Parker, W.D., Mills, C.J., De Fruyt, F., & Mervielde, I. (2002).
Personality trait development from age 12 to age 18: Longitudinal, cross-sectional and cross-cultural analyses. *Journal of Personality and Social Psychology, 83*(6), 1456.

McCrae, R.R., & Sutin, A.R. (2009).
Openness to experience. New York, NY: Guilford Press.

McGuire, W.J., McGuire, C.V., Child, P., & Fujioka, T. (1978).
Salience of ethnicity in the spontaneous self-concept as a function of one's ethnic distinctiveness in the social environment. *Journal of Personality and Social Psychology, 36*(5), 511-520.

McGuire, W.J., & Padawer-Singer, A. (1976).
Trait salience in the spontaneous self-concept. *Journal of Personality and Social Psychology, 33*(6), 743-754.

McKnight, P.E., & Kashdan, T.B. (2009).
The importance of functional impairment to mental health outcomes: A case for reassessing our goals in depression treatment research. *Clinical Psychology Review, 29*(3), 243-259.

Mezirow, J. (1985).
A critical theory of self-directed learning. In S. Brookfield (Ed.), *New directions for adult and continuing education* (pp. 17-30). San Francisco, CA: Jossey-Bass.

Mezirow, J. (2000).
Learning to think like an adult: Core concepts of transformation theory. In J. Mezirow & Associates (Eds.), *Learning as transformation: Critical perspectives on a theory in progress* (pp. 3-34). San Francisco, CA: Jossey-Bass.

MHA Labs (2014).
MHA Building Blocks. Retrieved from http://mhalabs.org/blog/2013/06/18/mha-building-blocks/

Mikva Challenge (2014).
Program impact spotlight: Expunge.io. Retrieved from https://www.mikvachallenge.org/blog/program-impact-spotlight-expunge-io/

Mischel, W., Cantor, N., & Feldman, S. (1996).
Principles of self-regulation: The nature of willpower and self-control. In E.T. Higgins & A.W. Kruglanski (Eds.), *Social psychology: Handbook of basic principles* (pp. 329-360). New York, NY: Guilford Press.

Mischel, W., Shoda, Y., & Peake, P.K. (1988).
The nature of adolescent competencies predicted by preschool delay of gratification. *Journal of Personality and Social Psychology, 54*(4), 687.

Moffitt, T.E. (1993).
Adolescence-limited and life-course-persistent antisocial behavior: A developmental taxonomy. *Psychological Review, 100*(4), 674.

Moffitt, T.E. (2003).
Life-course-persistent and adolescence-limited antisocial behavior: a 10-year research review and a research agenda. In T.E.M.B.B. Lahey & A. Caspi (Ed.), *Causes of conduct disorder and juvenile delinquency* (pp. 49-75). New York, NY: Guilford Press.

Moffitt, T.E., Arseneault, L., Belsky, D., Dickson, N., Hancox, R. J., Harrington, H., . . . Ross, S. (2011).
A gradient of childhood self-control predicts health, wealth, and public safety. *Proceedings of the National Academy of Sciences, 108*(7), 2693-2698.

Moilanen, K.L. (2007).
The adolescent self-regulatory inventory: The development and validation of a questionnaire of short-term and long-term self-regulation. *Journal of Youth and Adolescence, 36*(6), 835-848.

Montemayor, R., & Eisen, M. (1977).
The development of self-conceptions from childhood to adolescence. *Developmental Psychology, 13*(4), 314-319.

Moroney, D., Newman, J., Smith, C., McGovern, G., & Yohalem, N. (2014).
Understanding key elements, processes, and outcomes of expanded learning systems: A Review of the literature. New York, NY: Every Hour Counts.

Morrison, F.J., Ponitz, C.C., & McClelland, M.M. (2010).
Self-regulation and academic achievement in the transition to school. In S.D. Calkins & M.A. Bell (Eds.), *Child Development at the Intersection of Emotion and Cognition* (pp. 203-224). Washington, DC: American Psychological Association.

Moshman, D. (2005).
Adolescent psychological development: Rationality, morality, and identity, 2nd ed. Mahwah, NJ: Lawrence Erlbaum Associates.

Mueller, C.M., & Dweck, C.S. (1998).
Praise for intelligence can undermine children's motivation and performance. *Journal of Personality and Social Psychology, 75*(1), 33-52.

National Center for O*NET Development (2014).
*The O*Net Content Model.* Retrieved from http://www.onetcenter.org/content.html

National Governors' Association Center for Best Practices, Council of Chief State School Officers (2010).
Common Core State Standards. Washington, DC: Authors.

National Research Council (1984).
Development during middle childhood: The years from six to twelve. Washington, DC: National Academies.

National Research Council and Institute of Medicine. (2000).
From Neurons to Neighborhoods: The Science of Early Childhood Development. Committee on Integrating the Science of Early Childhood Development. In J. P. Shonkoff & D. A. Phillips (Eds.), Board on Children, Youth, and Families, Division of Behavioral and Social Sciences and Education. Washington, DC: National Academy Press.

National Research Council and Institute of Medicine. (2002).
Community Programs to Promote Youth Development. Committee Community-Level Programs for Youth. In J. Eccles & J. Appleton Gootman (Eds.), Board on Children, Youth, and Families, Commission on Behavioral and Social Sciences and Education. Washington, DC: National Academy Press.

Neal, J.W., & Neal, Z.P. (2013).
Nested or networked? Future directions for ecological systems theory. *Social Development, 22*(4), 722-737.

Nicholls, J.G., & Miller, A.T. (1984).
Reasoning about the ability of self and others: A developmental study. *Child Development, 55*(6), 1990-1999.

Noftle, E.E., & Robins, R.W. (2007).
Personality predictors of academic outcomes: Big five correlates of GPA and SAT scores. *Journal of Personality and Social Psychology, 93*(1), 116-130.

Office of Head Start, Administration for Children and Families, U.S. Department of Health and Human Services (2011).
The Head Start child development and early learning framework. Promoting positive outcomes in early childhood programs serving children 3-5 years old. Washington, DC: Author. Retrieved from https://eclkc.ohs.acf.hhs.gov/hslc/tta-system/teaching/eecd/Assessment/Child%20Outcomes/HS_Revised_Child_Outcomes_Framework%28rev-Sept2011%29.pdf

Olivola, C.Y., & Shafir, E. (2013).
The martyrdom effect: When pain and effort increase prosocial contributions. *Journal of Behavioral Decision Making, 26*(1), 91-105.

Oyserman, D. (2001).
Self-concept and identity. In A. Tesser & N. Schwarz (Eds.), *The Blackwell handbook of social psychology* (pp. 499-517). Malden, MA: Blackwell.

Oyserman, D. (2008).
Racial-ethnic self-schemas: Multi-dimensional identity-based motivation. *Journal of Research in Personality, 42*(5), 1186-1198.

Oyserman, D., Bybee, D., & Terry, K. (2006).
Possible selves and academic outcomes: How and when possible selves impel action. *Journal of Personality and Social Psychology, 91*(1), 188-204.

Oyserman, D., & Fryberg, S. A. (2006).
The possible selves of diverse adolescents: Content and function across gender, race, and national origin. In C. Dunkel & J. Kerpelman (Eds.), *Possible selves: Theory, research, and application* (pp. 17-39). Huntington, NY: Nova.

Oyserman, D., & James, L. (2011).
Possible identities. In S. Schwartz, K. Luyckx, & V. Vignoles (Eds.), *Handbook of identity theory and research* (pp. 117-145). New York, NY: Springer Science+Business Media, LLC.

Oyserman D., & Markus, H.R. (1998).
Self as social representation. In U. Flick (Ed.), *The psychology of the social* (pp. 107-125). New York, NY: Cambridge University Press.

Oyserman, D., & Markus, H. (1990).
Possible selves in balance: Implications for delinquency. *Journal of Social Issues, 46*(2), 141-157.

Oyserman, D., Terry, K., & Bybee, D. (2002).
A possible selves intervention to enhance school involvement. *Journal of Adolescence, 25*(3), 313-326.

Osterman, K.F. (2000).
Students' need for belonging in the school community. *Review of Educational Research, 70*(3), 323-367.

Ozer, D.J., & Benet-Martinez, V. (2006).
Personality and the prediction of consequential outcomes. *Annual Review Psychology, Annual Reviews, 57,* 401-421.

Palincsar, A., & Brown, A. (1984).
Reciprocal teaching of comprehension-fostering and comprehension-monitoring activities. *Cognition and Instruction, 1*(2), 117-175.

Pajares, F. (1996).
Self-efficacy beliefs in academic settings. *Review of Educational Research, 66*(4), 543-578.

Parker, J.G., & Asher, S.R. (1987).
Peer relations and later personal adjustment: Are low-accepted children at risk? *Psychological Bulletin, 102*(3), 357.

Partnership for 21st Century Skills (2009).
P21 framework definitions. Retrieved from http://www.p21.org/storage/documents/P21_Framework_Definitions.pdf

Patton, D.U. (2012).
Connected, known, and protected: African American adolescent males navigating community violence (Doctoral dissertation). University of Chicago. ProQuest document ID 1040725746.

Patton, D. (2013).
Between two worlds: Resilient African American adolescent males navigating community violence. In M. Harris (Ed.), *African American perspectives: Family dynamics, health care issues and the role of ethnicity* (pp. 87-102). Hauppauge, NY: Nova Science Publishers.

Pellegrino, J.W., & Hilton, M.L. (2012).
Education for life and work: Developing transferable knowledge and skills in the 21st century. Washington, DC: National Academies Press.

Perry, B.D. (2001).
The neuroarchaeology of childhood maltreatment: The neuro-developmental costs of adverse childhood events. In K. Franey, R. Geffner, & R. Falconer (Eds.), *The cost of child maltreatment: Who pays? We all do* (pp. 15-37). San Diego, CA: Family Violence and Sexual Assault Institute.

Perry, B. (2006).
Applying principles of neurodevelopment to clinical work with maltreated and traumatised children. In N. Boyd Webb (Ed.). *Working with Traumatised Youth in Child Welfare* (pp. 27-52).

Petersen, I.T., Bates, J.E., & Staples, A.D. (2015).
The role of language ability and self-regulation in the development of inattentive-hyperactive behavior problems. *Development and Psychopathology, 27,* 221-237. New York, NY: Guilford Press.

Philliber Research Associates. (2013).
Beyond content: Incorporating social and emotional learning into the strive framework (Vol. I): Social and emotional competencies and their relationship to academic achievement. Accord, NY: StriveTogether.

Phillips, T.M., & Pittman, J.F. (2003).
Identity processes in poor adolescents: Exploring the linkages between economic disadvantage and the primary task of adolescence. *Identity: An International Journal of Theory and Research, 3*(2), 115-129.

Phinney, J.S. (1989).
Stages of ethnic identity development in minority group adolescents. *The Journal of Early Adolescence, 9*(1-2), 34-49.

Phinney, J.S., & Rosenthal, D.A. (1992).
Ethnic identity in adolescence: Process, context, and outcome. In G.R. Adams, T.P. Gullotta, & R. Montemayor (Eds.), *Adolescent identity formation* (pp. 145-172). Newbury Park, CA: Sage.

Piaget, J. (1946/1951).
Play, dreams and imitation in children. New York, NY: Norton.

Piaget, J. (1952).
The origins of intelligence in children. New York, NY: International Universities Press.

Piaget, J. (1970).
Piaget's theory. In P.H. Mussen (Ed.), *Carmichael's Manual of Child Psychology* (3rd ed.) (pp. X-Y). New York, NY: John Wiley & Sons, Inc.

Ponitz, C.C., McClelland, M.M., Matthews, J.S., & Morrison, F.J. (2009).
A structured observation of behavioral self-regulation and its contribution to kindergarten outcomes. *Developmental Psychology, 45*(3), 605-619.

Pritchard, J. (2013).
The importance of soft skills in entry-level employment and postsecondary success: Perspectives from employers and community colleges. Seattle, OR: Seattle Jobs Initiative. Retrieved from http://www.seattlejobsinitiative.com/wp-content/uploads/SJI_SoftSkillsReport_vFINAL_1.17.13.pdf

Putnam, R. (2015).
Our kids: The American Dream in crisis. New York, NY: Simon & Schuster.

Rachlin, H., & Brown, J., & Cross, D. (2000).
Discounting in judgment of delay and probability. *Journal of Behavioral Decision Making, 13,* 145-159.

Raver, C.C., & Knitze, J. (2002).
Ready to enter: What research tells policymakers about strategies to promote social and emotional school readiness among three- and four-year-old children. New York, NY: National Center for Children in Poverty, Mailman School of Public Health, Columbia University.

Reardon, S.F. (2011).
The widening academic achievement gap between the rich and the poor: New evidence and possible explanations. In R. Murnane & G. Duncan (Eds.), *Whither opportunity? Rising inequality and the uncertain life chances of low-income children* (pp. 91-116). New York, NY: Russell Sage Foundation.

Rimm-Kaufman, S.E., Pianta, R.C., & Cox, M.J. (2000).
Teachers' judgments of problems in the transition to kindergarten. *Early Childhood Research Quarterly, 15*(2), 147-166.

Rogers, C.R. (1959).
A theory of therapy, personality, and interpersonal relationships, as developed in the client-centered framework. In S. Koch (Ed.), *Psychology: A study of science* (Vol. 13) (pp. 184-256). New York, NY: McGraw Hill.

Rokeach, M. (1971).
The measurement of values and value systems. In G. Abcarian & J.W. Soule (Eds.), *Social psychology and political behavior* (pp. X-Y). Columbus, OH: Charles Merrill.

Rosenberg, M. (1979).
Conceiving the self. New York, NY: Basic Books.

Rote, W.M., & Smetana, J.G. (2014).
Parenting, adolescent–parent relationships, and social domain theory: Implications for identity development. In K.C. McLean & M. Syed (Eds.), T*he Oxford handbook of identity development* (pp. 437-450). New York, NY: Oxford University Press.

Rotter, J.B. (1990).
Internal versus external control of reinforcement: A case history of a variable. *American psychologist, 45*(4), 489.

Rowe, M.L. (2008).
Child-directed speech: Relation to socioeconomic status, knowledge of child development and child vocabulary skill. *Journal of Child Language, 35*(1), 185-205.

Ruble, D.N. (1983).
The development of social comparison processes and their role in achievement-related self-socialization. *Social cognition and social development: A sociocultural perspective,* 134-157.

Ryan, R.M., & Deci, E.L. (2000).
Intrinsic and extrinsic motivations: Classic definitions and new directions. *Contemporary Educational Psychology, 25*(1), 54-67.

Ryan, R.M., & Deci, E.L. (2006).
Autonomy: Does psychology need choice, self-determination, and will? *Journal of Personality, 74*(6), 1557-1586.

Sansone, C., Weir, C., Harpster, L., Morgan, C. (1992).
Once a boring task always a boring task? *Journal of Personality and Social Psychology, 63*(3), 379.

95

Savitz-Romer, M., & Bouffard, S. (2012).
Ready, willing, and able: A developmental approach to college access and success. Cambridge, MA: Harvard Education Press.

Scales, P.C., Benson, P.L., & Roehlkepartain, E.C. (2011). Adolescent thriving: The role of sparks, relationships, and empowerment. *Journal of Youth and Adolescence, 40*(3), 263-277.

Scardamalia, M., Bereiter, C., & Steinbach, R. (1984). Teachability of reflective processes in written composition. *Cognitive Science, 8*(2), 173-190.

Schunk, D.H., & Meece, J.L. (2006).
Self-efficacy development in adolescence. In F. Pajares & T. Urdan (Eds.), *Self-efficacy beliefs of adolescents* (pp. 971-96). Greenwich, CT: Information Age Publishing.

Schunk, D.H., & Mullen, C.A. (2012).
Self-efficacy as an engaged learner. In S.L. Christenson, A.L. Reschly, & C. Wylie (Eds), *Handbook of research on student engagement* (pp. 219-235). New York: Springer Science+Business Media, LLC.

Schoenfeld, A.H. (1983).
Problem solving in the mathematics curriculum: A report, recommendation, and an annotated bibliography (MMA Notes #1). Washington, DC: Mathematical Association of America.

Schoenfeld, A.H. (1985).
Mathematical problem solving. Orlando, FL: Academic Press.

Schoenfeld, A.H. (1991).
On mathematics as sense-making: An informal attack on the unfortunate divorce of formal and informal mathematics. In J.F. Voss, D.N. Perkins, & J.W. Segal (Eds.), *Informal Reasoning and Education* (pp. 311-343). Hillsdale, NY: Lawrence Erlbaum Associates, Inc.

Schwartz, S.J., Côté, J.E., & Arnett, J.J. (2005).
Identity and agency in emerging adulthood: Two developmental routes in the individualization process. *Youth & Society, 37*(2), 201-229.

Schweinhart, L.J., Montie, J., Xiang, Z., Barnett, W.S., Belfield, C.R., & Nores, M. (2005).
Lifetime effects: The HighScope Perry Preschool study through age 40. (Monographs of the HighScope Educational Research Foundation, 14). Ypsilanti, MI: HighScope Press.

Search Institute. (2014).
A research update from Search Institute: Developmental relationships. Minneapolis, MN: Author. Retrieved from http://www.search-institute.org/what-we-study/developmental-relationships

Seligman, M.E.P. (1972).
Learned helplessness. *Annual Review of Medicine, 23,* 407-412.

Shih, M., Pittinsky, T.L., & Ambady, N. (1999).
Stereotype susceptibility: Identity salience and shifts in quantitative performance. *Psychological Science, 10*(1), 80-83.

Shoda, Y., Mischel, W., & Peake, P.K. (1990).
Predicting adolescent cognitive and self-regulatory competencies from preschool delay of gratification: Identifying diagnostic conditions. *Development Psychology, 26*(6), 978-986.

Shonkoff, J.P. (2011).
Protecting brains, not simply stimulating minds. *Science, 333*(6045), 982-983.

Shonkoff, J.P., Garner, A.S., Siegel, B.S., Dobbins, M.I., Earls, M.F., McGuinn, L., Pasco, J., & Wood, D.L. (2012). The lifelong effects of early childhood adversity and toxic stress. *Pediatrics, 129*(1), e232-e246.

Shulman, S., Laursen, B., Kalman, Z., & Karpovsky, S. (1997). Adolescent intimacy revisited. *Journal of Youth in Adolescence, 26*(5), 597-617.

Smith, J. (2003).
The making of young lives with/against the school credential. *Journal of Education and Work, 16*(2), 127-146.

Smyth, J., & Hattam, R. (2001).
"Voiced" research as a sociology for understanding "dropping out" of school. *British Journal of Sociology of Education, 22*(3), 401-415.

Stanton-Salazar, R.D. (2011).
A social capital framework for the study of institutional agents and their role in the empowerment of low-status students and youth. *Youth & Society, 43*(3), 1066-1109.

Steele, C.M. (1997).
A threat in the air: How stereotypes shape intellectual identity and performance. *American Psychologist, 52*(6), 613-629.

Steele, C.M., & Aronson, J. (1995).
Stereotype threat and the intellectual test performance of African Americans. *Journal of Personality and Social Psychology, 69*(5), 797-811.

Stefanou, C.R., Perencevich, K.C., DiCintio, M., & Turner, J.C. (2004).
Supporting autonomy in the classroom: Ways teachers encourage student decision making and ownership. *Educational Psychologist, 39*(4), 97-110.

Steinberg, L. (2005).
Cognitive and affective development in adolescence. *Trends in Cognitive Sciences, 9*(2), 69-74.

Steinberg, L. (2007).
Risk taking in adolescence new perspectives from brain and behavioral science. *Current Directions in Psychological Science, 16*(2), 55-59.

96

Steinberg, L., & Morris, A.S. (2001). Adolescent development. *Annual Review of Psychology, 52,* 83-110.

Stetser, M., & Stillwell, R. (2014). *Public High School Four-Year On-Time Graduation Rates and Event Dropout Rates: School Years 2010-11 and 2011-12. First Look (NCES 2014-391).*

Stipek, D. (2004). *Engaging schools: Fostering high school students' motivation to learn.* Washington, DC: National Research Council, National Academy Press.

Stipek, D., & Gralinski, J.H. (1996). Children's beliefs about intelligence and school performance. *Journal of Educational Psychology, 88*(3), 397.

Susman, S., Dent, C., McAdams, L., Stacy, A., Burton D., & Flay, B. (1994). Group self-identification and adolescent cigarette smoking: A 1-year prospective study. *Journal of Abnormal Psychology, 103*(3), 576–80.

Swann, W. (1997). The trouble with change: Self-verification and allegiance to the self. *Psychological Science, 8*(3), 177-180.

Tangney, J.P., Baumeister, R.F., & Boone, A.L. (2004). High self-control predicts good adjustment, less pathology, better grades, and interpersonal success. *Journal of Personality, 72*(2), 271-324.

Tett, R.P., Jackson, D.N., & Rothstein, M. (1991). Personality measures as predictors of job performance: a meta-analytic review. *Personnel psychology, 44*(4), 703-742.

Thaler, R., & Shefrin, H. (1981). An economic theory of self-control. *Journal of Political Economy, 89*(2), 392-406.

Thompson, R.A. (2008). Early attachment and later development: Familiar questions, new answers. In J. Cassidy & P.R. Shaver (Eds.), *Handbook of attachment: Theory, research, and clinical applications* (2nd ed.) (pp. 348-365). New York, NY: Guilford Press.

Tinto, V. (1997). Colleges as communities: Taking research on student persistence seriously. *The Review of Higher Education, 21*(2), 167-177.

Trope, Y., & Fishbach, A. (2000). Counteractive self-control in overcoming temptation. *Journal of Personality and Social Psychology, 79*(4), 493-506.

University of Chicago Crime Lab (July 13, 2012). *BAM–Sports Edition.* Retrieved from https://crimelab.uchicago.edu/sites/crimelab.uchicago.edu/files/uploads/BAM_FINAL%20Research%20and%20Policy%20Brief_20120711.pdf

U.S. Department of Education. (n.d.). Washington, DC: National Center for Education Statistics. Retrieved from http://nces.ed.gov/pubsearch

U.S. Department of Education. (2012). *Advancing civic learning and engagement in democracy: A road map and call to action.* Washington, DC: U.S. Department of Education.

U.S. White House, Office of the Press Secretary. (2009, April 24). Remarks by the President on higher education. Retrieved from https://www.whitehouse.gov/the_press_office/Remarks-by-the-President-on-Higher-Education

U.S. White House, Office of the Press Secretary. (2009, February 24). Presidential address to joint session of Congress. Retrieved from https://www.whitehouse.gov/the_press_office/Remarks-of-President-Barack-Obama-Address-to-Joint-Session-of-Congress

Ungar, M. (2004). A constructivist discourse on resilience. Multiple contexts, multiple realities among at-risk children and youth. *Youth & Society, 35*(3), 341-365.

Vedder-Weiss, D., & Fortuc, D. (2011). Adolescents' declining motivation to learn science: Inevitable or not? *Journal of Research in Science Teaching, 48*(2), 199-216.

Vygotsky, L. (1962). *Thought and language.* Oxford, UK: Wiley.

Vygotsky, L. (1978). *Interaction between learning and development. Mind and society.* Cambridge, MA: Harvard University Press.

Wagner, T., & Compton, R.A. (2012). *Creating innovators: The making of young people who will change the world.* New York, NY: Scribner.

Watson, M.W. (1981). The development of social roles: A sequence of social-cognitive development. *New Directions for Child and Adolescent Development, 1981*(12), 33-41.

Weber, J. (1993). Exploring the relationship between personal values and moral reasoning. *Human Relations, 46*(4), 435-463.

Weick, K.E. (1995). *Sensemaking in organizations.* Thousand Oaks, CA: Sage Publications.

Weinstock, M. (2005). The potential influence of maternal stress hormones on development and mental health of the offspring. *Brain, Behavior and Immunity, 19*(4), 296-308.

Weisberg, D.S., & Gopnik, A. (2013). Pretense, counterfactuals, and Bayesian causal models: Why what is not real really matters. *Cognitive Science, 37*(4), 1368-1381.

97

Weissberg, R.P., & Cascarino, J. (2013). Academic learning + social-emotional learning = national priority. *Phi Delta Kappan, 95*(2), 8-13.

Wellman, H.M., Cross, D., & Watson, J. (2001). Meta-analysis of theory-of-mind development: The truth about false belief. *Child Development, 72*(3), 655-684.

Wethington, H.R., Hahn, R.A., Fuqua-Whitley, D.S. ... Task Force on Community Preventive Services. (2008). The effectiveness of interventions to reduce psychological harm from traumatic events among children and adolescents: a systematic review. *American Journal of Preventive Medicine, 35*(3), 287-313.

White, K.S., Bruce, S.E., Farrell, A.D., & Kliewer, W. (1998). Impact of exposure to community violence on anxiety: A longitudinal study of family social support as a protective factor for urban children. *Journal of Child and Family Studies, 7*(2), 187-203.

Wigfield, A. (1994). Expectancy-value theory of achievement motivation: A developmental perspective. *Education Psychology Review, 6*(1), 49-78.

Wigfield, A., Eccles, J. (1992). The development of achievement task values: A theoretical analysis. *Developmental Review, 12*(3), 265-310.

Wilson, W.J. (1990). *The truly disadvantaged: The inner city, the underclass, and public policy.* Chicago, IL: University of Chicago Press.

Wilson, W.J. (2012). *The declining significance of race: Blacks and changing American institutions.* Chicago, IL: University of Chicago Press.

Winstein, C. (2014, April 9). *Does practice make perfect?* Retrieved from http://www.brainfacts.org/about-neuroscience/ask-an-expert/articles/2014/does-practice-make-perfect/

Wrzesniewski, A., Dutton, J.E., & Debebe, G. (2003). Interpersonal sensemaking and the meaning of work. *Research in Organizational Behavior, 25,* 93-135.

Yeager, D.S., Henderson, M.D., Paunesku, D., Walton, G.M., D'Mello, S., Spitzer, B.J., Duckworth, A.L. (2014). Boring but important: A self-transcendent purpose for learning fosters academic self-regulation. *Journal of Personality and Social Psychology, 107*(4), 559-580.

Yeager, D., & Walton, G. (2011). Social-psychological interventions in education: They're not magic. *Review of Educational Research, 81*(2), 267-301.

Yoshikawa, H., Aber, J.L., & Beardslee, W.R. (2012). The effects of poverty on the mental, emotional, and behavioral health of children and youth: Implications for prevention. *American Psychologist, 67*(4), 272-284.

Zimmerman, B.J. (2002). Becoming a self-regulated learner: An overview. *Theory into practice, 41*(2), 64-70.

Zimmerman, B.J., & Cleary, T.J. (2006). Adolescents' development of personal agency: The role of self-efficacy beliefs and self-regulatory skill. In F. Pajares & T.C. Urdan (Eds.), *Self-efficacy beliefs of adolescents* (Vol. 5) (pp. 45-69). Charlotte, NC: Information Age Publishing.

Zimmerman, B.J., & Ringle, J. (1981). Effects of model persistence and statements of confidence on children's self-efficacy and problem solving. *Journal of Educational Psychology, 73*(4), 485-493.

Appendix

TABLE A.1

List of Experts Who Provided Input and Feedback Throughout This Project

Name	Organization	Title
Barbara Abel	Educare of Chicago/Ounce of Prevention Fund	Birth to Five Curriculum Specialist
Rashida Abuwala	Boys Clubs of NYC	Chief Program Officer
Stephanie Alyward	University of Chicago	Child Assessor
Dana Ansel		Research and Evaluation Consultant
Melissa Authement	Polaris Charter Academy	Founding Teacher; Instructional Guide
Abigail Baird	Vasser College	Associate Professor of Psychology
Sara Bartolino	Transforming Education	Co-Founder and Executive Director
Rhonda Bell	Gary Comer Youth Center	Director
Sanee Bell	Katy (TX) Independent School District	Principal
Leslie Beller	MHA Labs	Director and Founder (MHA)
Ron Berger	Expeditionary Learning	Chief Academic Officer
Harry Berman	Illinois Board of Higher Education	Executive Director
Melinda Berry	Educare of Chicago/Ounce of Prevention Fund	Senior Family Support Specialist
Jessica Besser-Rosenberg	One Million Degrees	Director, Research and Communications
Suzanne Bouffard	Harvard Graduate School of Education	Researcher
Sarah Bowie	SGA Youth and Family Services	Check & Connect Manager
Daniela Boykin	CUNY ASAP	Deputy Director
Betsy Brand	American Youth Policy Forum	Executive Director
Chris Broughton	Cristo Rey Network	Senior Director of College Initiatives
Chris Brown	Elev8 Chicago	Director of Education and Engagement
Kat Bryant	Capitol Hill Day School	Middle School Teacher
Amanda Cage	Chicago Cook Workforce Partnership	Director of Strategic Initiatives and Policy
Dan Cardinali	Communities in Schools	President
Barbara Cervone	What Kids Can Do	Founder and President
Sandra Christenson	University of Minnesota	Professor
Tonya Cody-Robinson	Chicago Cook Workforce Partnership	Project Coordinator
Deloria Collins	SGA Youth and Family Services	Check & Connect Monitor
Lauren Collins	The Lab School, University of Chicago	Early Childhood Education Administrator
Denise Conkright	PACT	Executive Director
David Conley	University of Oregon, College of Education	Professor; Director, Center for Educational Policy Research
James Côté	University of Western Ontario	Professor, Department of Sociology
Philip Courtney	Urban Arts Partnership	Founder
Rachel Cytron	Harlem RBI	Associate Executive Director
Greg Darnieder	U.S. Department of Education	Senior Advisor
Joyce Debrah-Sheppard	Chicago Public Schools	Social and Emotional Learning Specialist
Regina Deil-Amen	University of Arizona	Associate Professor, Center for the Study of Higher Education

Name	Organization	Title
Aarti Dhupelia	Chicago Public Schools	Chief Officer, College and Career Success
Angela Diaz	Mount Sinai Hospital	Jean C. and James W. Crystal Professor, Departments of Pediatrics and Preventive Medicine; Director, Adolescent Health Center
Larry Dieringer	Engaging Schools	Executive Director
Jessica Donner	Every Hour Counts	Director
Michael Driscoll	Changing Worlds	Manager of After-School and Community Outreach Programs
Mark Duhon	HighSight	Founder and Executive Director
Kelly Dwyer	Spark	Chief Knowledge Officer
Jacquelynne Eccles	University of California-Irvine	Distinguished Professor of Education
Brenda Eiland-Williford	Ounce of Prevention Fund	Director of Program and Curricula
Crystal Elliott-O'Connor	Family Focus, Inc.	Associate Director, Early Childhood Development Programs
Sandra Escamilla	Youth Development Institute	Executive Director
Susan Farrugia	University of Illinois at Chicago	Assistant Vice Provost, Undergraduate Affairs
Ron Ferguson	Harvard Graduate School of Education	Senior Lecturer in Education and Public Policy
Connie Flanagan	University of Wisconsin-Madison	Professor, School of Human Ecology
Ernestine Fleming-Jones	Kenwood Academy	Attendance Coordinator
Nilda Flores-Gonzalez	University of Illinois at Chicago	Associate Professor, Department of Sociology
Ellen Galinsky	Families and Work Institute	President and Co-Founder
Kathleen Gallagher	University of North Carolina at Chapel Hill	Clinical Assistant Professor
Ruth Genn	Bottom Line	Executive Director, NYC Office
Fakelia Guyton	Family Focus, Evanston	Program Manager
Reginald Halbert	Dunbar High School	Teacher
Lucy Hall	Jumpstart	Site Coordinator
Robert Halpern	Erikson Institute	Professor
Bridget Hamre	University of Virginia, Curry School of Education	Associate Director and Research Associate Professor, Center for Advanced Study of Teaching and Learning
Marcia Hanlon	Associated Colleges of Illinois	Director, College Readiness & Completion
Colleen Harvey	Playworks	Program Director
Keith Hefner	Youth Communication	Executive Director
Carrie Heller	Circus Arts Institute	Founder and Executive Director
Mary Louise Hemmeter	Vanderbilt University	Professor, Department of Special Education; Faculty Director of the Susan Gray School for Children
Lucy Herz	Student Success Network	Program Director
Lori Hill	University of Michigan	Assistant Professor
Harry Holzer	Georgetown University	Professor, Public Policy
Stephanie Jones	Harvard Graduate School of Education	Marie and Max Kargman Associate Professor in Human Development and Urban Education
Kasumi Kato	CircEsteem	Coordinator
Leeandra Khan	Bronzeville Scholastic Institute	Principal
Michael Kristovic	University of Chicago School of Social Service Administration, Network for College Success	Adjunct Lecturer and Social and Academic Supports Facilitator
Jiffy Lansing	Chapin Hall	Researcher
Lila Leff	UMOJA Student Development Corporation	Founder